THE MALTESE

Diane Morgan

The Maltese

Project Team
Editor: Heather Russell-Revesz
Copy Editor: Lexiann Grant
Design: Angela Stanford
Series Design: Stephanie Krautheim
Series Originator: Dominique De Vito

T.F.H. Publications
President/CEO: Glen S. Axelrod
Executive Vice President: Mark E. Johnson
Publisher: Christopher T. Reggio
Production Manager: Kathy Bontz

T.F.H. Publications, Inc.
One TFH Plaza
Third and Union Avenues
Neptune City, NJ 07753

06 07 08 09 10 1 3 5 7 9 8 6 4 2
Printed and bound in China

Library of Congress Cataloging-in-Publication Data
Morgan, Diane, 1947-
  The Maltese / Diane Morgan.
     p. cm.
  Includes index.
  ISBN 0-7938-3637-9 (alk. paper)
  1. Maltese dog. I. Title.
  SF429.M25M67 2006
  636.76—dc22
  2005037453

This book has been published with the intent to provide accurate and authoritative information in regard to the subject matter within. While every precaution has been taken in preparation of this book, the author and publisher expressly disclaim responsibility for any errors, omissions, or adverse effects arising from the use or application of the information contained herein. The techniques and suggestions are used at the reader's discretion and are not to be considered a substitute for veterinary care. If you suspect a medical problem consult your veterinarian.

The Leader In Responsible Animal Care For Over 50 Years.™
www.tfhpublications.com

TABLE OF CONTENTS

1

HISTORY
of the Maltese

W hile the origins of domestic dogs are shrouded in mystery, one thing is sure: Your Maltese used to be a wolf. It seems like a far stretch, but the fact is that they are one species. It's odd to think of the delicate and sophisticated Maltese sharing the appetites and habits of the wolf, but it's true nonetheless. In fact, all present day dogs, from the Maltese to the Malamute, are descended from the gray wolf. They share one blood and one heritage. They have the same genetic makeup, like the same food, understand the same body language, and have similar social structures—a pack. But while the wolfpack is made up of other wolves, the Maltese has chosen to share his life with you, his human family. And it was his choice. Human beings did not domesticate the wolves. On the contrary, certain wolves, bolder than the rest of the pack, sought us out; they chose the fireside, the company, and the leftovers over the wind and the cold. It was a daring bargain, and it worked for both of us.

Fossilized remains of the dog dating back to the Mesolithic period have been found along with the crude drawings of dogs on the caves. Most likely, the relationship between humans and dogs during this time was competitive, since both species survived on basically the same prey animals. Around 12,000 years ago people began to develop organized societies, and the domesticated dog developed right alongside of them. As the relationship deepened, these dogs began to rely on us for survival as their more wild traits, such as preying for food, were lost. The dog became dependent on people for food, and in return we became dependent on the dog for herding, working, hunting, and companionship.

The Maltese belongs to the "Toy Group" classification of dogs.

Thus, the symbiotic relationship between man and dog began.

Over thousands of years, many of the wolf-behavior genes went underground. These "wolves-turning-into-dogs" allowed themselves to be housetrained, to walk on a leash, and to be bathed. Their bodies changed in accordance to the tasks they were assigned. Sheep-herding dogs became hyper-reactive, guard-dogs turned their aggressive instincts against strangers, and toy dogs shrank in size and permitted themselves to be fondled by people who don't realize they have a wolf in their laps!

But as much as the Maltese is a wolf, he is something more. His genes may be those of a wolf, but it is with us humans he has cast his lot. The Maltese resembles us too—we even get the same diseases, including arthritis, obesity, diabetes, cancer, and psychiatric problems (in fact most of the gifts of old age and the settled life). We can infect each other with a host of ailments, from ringworm to scabies. We have the same feelings: depression, anger, joy, fear, jealousy, and boredom. We both can love devotedly and hate with a passion.

THE ORIGINS OF THE MALTESE

We probably know more about how wolves turned into dogs than how certain dogs evolved into the Maltese. Since this is a very, very ancient breed we have no records of who the first Maltese breeders were, or even where they were. Charles Darwin hazarded that the breed might be 6,000 years old, which if true, would make the Maltese the oldest breed known. However, most modern researchers agree that while the breed is old, it's probably not that old.

Where in the World?

Some historians place the origin of the breed in Malta. Others say Sicily, or perhaps Egypt or southern Europe. No one really knows, and part of the answer depends on whether you mean the Maltese-as-we-know-him-today or some far flung ancestor of the breed (in which case you might go right back to the wolf again). The truth is that the word "breed" is a pretty fluid concept. For many ancient people, a breed meant a type of dog who performed a special task. So a ratting dog might look like anything at all, so long as he caught rats. And a herding dog could have any sort of ear or coat or eye color, so long as he was able to herd sheep or cattle.

Later on, the word "breed" began to refer to a collection of dogs who looked alike within certain set limits and who behaved in certain ways. It also meant that you could mate these dogs to each other and have offspring who looked like the parents. In the Maltese, the salient characteristics are small, white, and very long-coated. So when we look back into history, what do we find that fits this bill?

It's hard to say. We have no photographs or even any technical descriptions, such as you'd find in today's breed standards. What we have are some drawings on vases and other art, a rather awful classical poem, and some remarks by Aristotle. (Other classical writers who referred to Maltese-like dogs included: Timon, Callimachus, Aelian, Artimidorus, Epaminodus, Martial, Strabo, Pliny Secundus, and Saint Clement of Alexandria, but Aristotle is the one who always gets quoted.)

Island Dogs?

Is the Maltese really from the island of Malta? Maybe. Malta may not seem like much of an island nowadays, but in its heyday, it was a major trading port in the Mediterranean, and dogs hailing from there could easily have found their way all over the ancient world. It was thought that the Maltese was bartered in exchange for food and supplies. Additionally, the Maltese could have been used as a means of protecting food rations on ships, since they are excellent at chasing and catching rodents, despite

Classifying Dogs

The American Kennel Club (AKC) divides dogs into seven groups for the purposes of dog shows: the Herding Group, the Working Group, the Sporting Group, the Hound Group, the Terrier Group, the Non-sporting Group, and the Toy Group. However, this classification is rather arbitrary, and the "nonsporting" group is really a miscellany of dogs. Deborah Lynch, a researcher at the Canine Studies Institute in Aurora, Ohio, believes a more useful categorization would divide dogs into sight hounds, scent hounds, working and guard dogs, northern dogs, flushing spaniels, water spaniels and retrievers, pointers, terriers, herding dogs, toy and companion dogs (that's our friend the Maltese, of course, although the club maintains that he has very terrier-like qualities as well!). Indeed, the Fédération Cynologique Internationale uses a very similar classification to Lynch's.

Aristotle wrote about Maltese-like dogs.

their fragile appearance.

Aristotle wrote "Canis Melitae, (the dog of Malta) is of the tiny sort, being perfectly proportioned, notwithstanding its very small size." From this, people have assumed that the modern Maltese is this very same dog. But it gets more complicated: There was also a town called Melitae, and perhaps the breed hailed from there! Certainly the town of Melitae was closer to Etruscan territory than the Isle of Malta. It can be frustrating when the evidence is not clear.

Greece and Rome

Strabo, the famous geographer, maintained that the breed came from Sicily. He wrote about these "tender little dogs, no bigger than ferrets, who yet are not small in understanding, nor changeable in their love." This is a tribute worthy of the breed.

At any rate, both Greeks and the Romans were very fond of their tiny white dogs, even erecting tombs to them when they died, with the inscription, "Offspring of the stock of Malta." At least that's what Theophrastus said, and he should know. Another inscription reads: "The stone on this spot commemorates the swift-footed Maltese, who was the faithful guardian of Eumelos." It's writings like these that make us wonder if we really are talking about the same breed here. Maltese are many things, but "swift-footed" is not the usual epithet applied to them. To make things even more muddled, the dog of the epitaph was named Bull. Somehow, "Bull" just doesn't sound like a Maltese-type name.

In addition, a vase found at the Etruscan city of Vulci dating to about 500 B.C.E depicts a small dog who resembles today's Maltese. To aid in the identification, the decipherable part of the text read "the guardians" followed by "Melitaie," or the dog of Melitians, suggesting the tiny dog was used as a guard, or at least as watch dog.

Egypt and Southern Europe

Other historians prefer to locate the origin of the breed in Egypt. Depictions of dogs closely resembling the modern Maltese, dating back to 600-300 B.C.E., have been found in Fayum, about the same time as Aristotle lived. The dogs were certainly popular there, and it's said that some of them were members of the royal family, achieving godlike status.

A southern European origin for the breed has its adherents also. Proponents of this theory claim that a spitz-like dog, bred for hunting in marshes and forests, was the true ancestor of the Maltese. If true, this may account for the "spaniel-like" appearance and temperament of the breed, and indeed at one time the Maltese was called "The Spaniel Gentle."

In any case, some believe, the dog accompanied his owners all over the known world, not just Malta, Italy, Greece, and Egypt, but even into the Far East and Tibet, where his genes gave rise to the Lhasa Apso, Tibetan Terrier, and even the Pekinese. This might seem far-fetched, but with a Maltese, one never knows—they are magical little dogs.

It's possible therefore that the "Canis Melitae" and the dogs of Egypt and other places were the same breed and the ancestors of the modern Maltese. However, it is also possible that the Maltese and Etruscan and Egyptian dogs were not the same breed and that only one of them—or none, or all—is the ancestor of our small white friend. It's that much of a mystery. (I don't even dare mention the name of the Baroness Wentworth here, who firmly maintained that the ancient dog of Malta looked more like a Pomeranian that anything else. And she researched the matter pretty thoroughly.)

Form and Function

Just as mysterious as the origins of the Maltese are the uses to which he was put. Some historians claim that the Maltese was always, first and foremost,

Issa, the Maltese

I suppose you might like to hear the poem, which is addressed to a Maltese dog named Issa. Issa belonged to the governor of Malta, a guy named Publius, who is said to have loved the dog more than life itself. The author is Marcus Martialis, more familiarly known, of course, as Martial.

> Issa is more frolicsome than Catulla's canary.
> Issa is more pure than a white dove's kiss.
> Issa is more gentle than a virgin maiden.
> Issa is more precious than jewels from India.
> Lest the days that she see light should snatch her from him forever,
> Publius has had her picture painted.

This picture, by the way, was supposed to have been so lifelike that that one could not tell the picture from the dog. Sadly, the portrait has not survived (neither has Issa).

Did You Know?

The Roman Emperor Claudius (10 B.C.E. – 54 C.E.) owned a Maltese.

a companion and lap dog—a true luxury item. It is well to remember, however, that even ancient lap dogs served a utilitarian purpose: to draw fleas from the dog's owner right onto the dog. (Ancient hygiene wasn't all it might be.) So you see that the old-time Maltese was very busy, even when he was just sitting in some society lady's lap. Others claim that the ancient Maltese was a mouser and ratter. Certainly today's Maltese is capable of catching a mouse, although I would hesitate to set one up against a big rat.

What's in a Name?

Even the name of the Maltese dog is disputed. From ancient times, the Maltese has been variously called the "Melitae Dog"; "Ye Ancient Dogge of Malta,"; "The Roman Ladies' Dog"; "Comforter,"; and the "Bichon," which is simply old French for "dog" and doesn't necessarily refer to the modern Bichon Frise. However—you guessed it—the Maltese is often cited as an ancestor of that breed too, and both breeds are sometimes classed as "Bichon-type" dogs.

Still other names include the "Maltese Lion Dog" and the "Shock" dog, not because of any electrical tendencies but merely referring to his distinctive shock of white hair. Most recently, the dog was called the "Maltese Terrier" before its name was finally shortened to simply "The Maltese."

ON TO ENGLAND

From ancient Egypt, to the Greek and Roman Empires, and into the reign of the British Empire, the Maltese has found his way onto the laps of the rich, wealthy, and powerful. There is evidence that the Maltese appeared in England during the reign of Henry VIII (1491-1547), where they were introduced to the homes of English aristocracy and, again, depicted in portraits on the laps of the ladies of the aristocracy.

Queen Elizabeth I (1533-1603) and Mary Queen of Scots (1542-1587) were owners of Maltese lap dogs. Dr. John Caius, a canine historian and the personal physician to Queen Elizabeth I, wrote this about the Maltese: "There is among us another kind of high bred dog … That kind is very small indeed, and chiefly sought after for the pleasure and amusement of women. The smaller the kind, the more pleasing it is, so that they carry them in their bosoms, in their beds, and in their arms while in their carriages."

Part of the dog's allure was that he was believed to have magical healing powers; the ailing person was instructed merely to place the dog on his or her chest or abdomen. This probably worked better than you might think. Modern science has shown that dogs produce a sense of well-being in people and actually do seem to help people get better faster. Besides, having a dog lie on your chest for an extended period of time is bound to make you want to get up sooner rather than later.

The English painter Sir Joshua Reynolds (1723-1792) painted a portrait of Nellie O'Brien holding a very Malty looking dog on her lap. O'Brien wasn't a member of the aristocracy, but she was Reynolds' favorite model and also probably his mistress. She was supposed be both intelligent and alluring. I have often wondered if he gave her the dog.

By the middle of the nineteenth century, the Maltese was firmly established as a pet dog in Britain. With the rise of dog shows and the establishment of the Kennel Club (KC) of the United Kingdom, the popularity of the Maltese was secured. The Maltese was among the first breeds to be entered into and exhibited at dog shows in the UK.

Show Dogs

While most owners of Maltese are mostly interested in owning a pet rather than a show dog, the Maltese is so stunning in the ring that any history of the breed should include mention of their history in the show ring. Showing dogs began as an "English thing," and the first dog show was put on to raise money for charity. This is no longer the case, but the early amateur breeders still set the standard for great dogs and good sportsmanship. Today, the prestigious British dog show, Crufts, is still a rather casual, family affair, unlike the glittering crowd you run into at the US's most famous dog show, Westminster.

The first dog show class for Maltese occurred in 1862, at the Agricultural Hall in London. Afterwards it was onward and upward, with the breed gaining in popularity until after World War I, when it suffered a decline. Now the breed is once again increasing in popularity.

THE MALTESE IN AMERICA

The Maltese seems to be historically prominent as an established breed entered into dog shows at the same time as his appearance in British dog shows. The first Maltese exhibited in America was entered into Westminster's first show in 1877, and was listed as the "Maltese Lion Dog." He was solid white and seemingly in close comparison to today's breed

Queen Elizabeth I and Mary Queen of Scots were owners of Maltese.

Maltese often win "Best in Show" at dog shows.

standard of the Maltese. Prior to this show, the first Maltese dog exhibited in 1873 in America was pure white with black ears. However, with the establishment of the American Kennel Club (AKC), Maltese registered from 1874 on were solid white (just as in the breed standard today). The American Kennel Club officially accepted the Maltese for registration in 1888, and the first registrants were two females charmingly named Topsy and Snips.

The first Maltese champion recorded by the American Kennel Club was named Thackery Rob Roy, owned by Mrs. C. S. Young. In 1912, the first Maltese won the title of Best in Show. He was named Sweetsir of Dyker, owned by Mrs. Carl Baumann.

During the 1940s Dr. Vincenzo Calvaresi was one of the most prominent members of the Maltese fancy in the US. With his Villa Malta breeding program he produced over 100 champions. In the 1950s, Toni and Aennchen Antonelli (Aennchen's Maltese kennel) were the main force in

establishing the Maltese breed in the US. One of their greatest champions was the lovely Ch. Aennchen's Poona Dancer, winner of 37 Best In Shows, owned by Larry Ward and the late Frank Oberstar.

Joanchenn's Maya Dancer, owned by Mamie Gregory, held the Best in Show winning record of 43 for Maltese (until recently broken in the 1990s by Ch. Sand Island Small Kraft Lite—Henry to his friends), bred and owned by the late Carol Frances Andersen and handled by Vicki Abbott. This dog amassed an astonishing 82 Bests in Show. But even this record was toppled by Ch. Ta-Jon's Tickle Me Silly, bred and handled by Tammy Simon and owned by Marion and Samuel Lawrence. She has 103 Best in Show wins, and is the current all-time top winning Maltese.

Today, the Maltese is one of the most popular breeds in the United States, with almost 14,000 registered every year with the AKC. Maltese shine at dog shows. In fact, this seems to be their favorite place—other than your lap, of course. They win often at shows, and while none has yet captured the title of Best in Show at Westminster, that day cannot be far away. They have already achieved Best in Group five times, most recently in 1992, and that alone is a difficult achievement.

Maltese of the Rich and Famous

The Maltese has always been favored by the glamorous: Elizabeth Taylor owned one named Sugar. Marilyn Monroe had her "Maf Honey," given to her by Frank Sinatra. Elvis Presley had Foxhugh, Tony Bennet had Boo, and Liberace owned three Maltese: Charmin, Solo, and Leah. The old-time actress Tallulah Bankhead owned Dolores. More contemporary Maltese-owning celebs include Heather Locklear with Harley, Halle Berry with Miss Polly and Little Willie, and Bryant Gumbel with Cujo. You never know about people, do you?

BREED CLUBS

In the mid-1800s, dog shows began to gain popularity. For the first time in the modern history of the dog, canines were not only being used as working dogs, hunting dogs, guard dogs, or companions, but for exhibition. Dogs and the breeding of dogs had become a hobby, a career, and even a passion for those in the Victorian era. While dogs had been informally referred to by breed names, there had never been a need to classify and cite the specific criteria of breed standards. With the emergence of dog shows, breed standards had become a necessity.

The Kennel Club of the United Kingdom

The Kennel Club (KC) was formed in 1873 in Great Britain by a group of dog show enthusiasts. The Kennel Club created breed standards by establishing stud books, setting standards for certain dog breeds, and establishing rules and regulations for dog shows. The Kennel Club's parentage was rooted in English formality and the strict standards set forth by the Kennel Club have continued to prevail in modern dog shows in England and abroad.

The Kennel Club of Great Britain led the way for the establishment of the American Kennel Club (AKC) in 1884 and the establishment of the Canadian Kennel Club (CKC) in 1888. Today, these clubs have a century plus of experience in educating owners, enforcing breed standards, keeping records on specific breeds and family lines, and conducting dog shows.

The American Kennel Club

The American Kennel Club was started on September 17, 1884 by a group of twelve dog show enthusiasts who saw the need for a national kennel club. They met at the

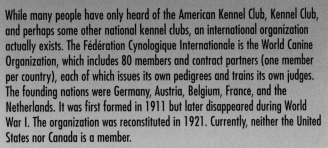

Fédération Cynologique Internationale

While many people have only heard of the American Kennel Club, Kennel Club, and perhaps some other national kennel clubs, an international organization actually exists. The Fédération Cynologique Internationale is the World Canine Organization, which includes 80 members and contract partners (one member per country), each of which issues its own pedigrees and trains its own judges. The founding nations were Germany, Austria, Belgium, France, and the Netherlands. It was first formed in 1911 but later disappeared during World War I. The organization was reconstituted in 1921. Currently, neither the United States nor Canada is a member.

The FCI ensures that its pedigrees and judges are recognized by all FCI members. Every member country conducts international shows as well as working trials; results are sent to the FCI office, where they are input into computers. When a dog has been awarded a certain number of awards, he can receive the title of International Beauty or Working Champion. These titles are confirmed by the FCI.

The FCI recognizes 331 dog breeds, and each of them is the "property" of a specific country, ideally the one in which the breed developed. The owner countries of the breeds write the standards for these breeds in cooperation with the Standards and Scientific Commissions of the FCI, and the translations and updates are carried out by the FCI.

In addition, via the national canine organization and the FCI, every breeder can ask for international protection of his or her kennel name.

Kennel clubs are a great place to learn about your favorite subject—Maltese!

Philadelphia Kennel Club in Pennsylvania. Each of these twelve men represented a dog club that had held a benched dog show in various cities throughout the eastern half of the United States. The second meeting of the newly formed American Kennel Club was held on October 22, 1884 at Madison Square Garden in New York City. A constitution was written, by-laws were adopted, and Major James M. Taylor was elected the American Kennel Club's first president. For the next three years, until 1887, meetings were held in various cities such as Cincinnati, Boston, Newark, New Jersey, and principally in New York. In 1887 a room was rented on 44 Broadway in New York City, and New York became the official home of the American Kennel Club's headquarters.

Today the AKC mantains a purebred dog registry, sanctions dog events, and promotes responsible dog ownership.

What Is a Breed Standard?

A breed standard is a set of guidelines that describe the ideal specimen of that breed. It is a written picture of the "perfect" dog from a particular breed.

The Canadian Kennel Club

While Americans are most familiar with their own AKC, Canada has its own breed registry: the Canadian Kennel Club (CKC), formed in 1888, which registers over 100,000 purebred dogs every year. The CKC runs shows and other canine events. It also publishes its own journal: *Dogs in Canada*. It provides all kinds of information and support for anyone interested in purebred dogs.

The American Maltese Association

The American Kennel Club recognizes the American Maltese Association as the national parent breed club for the Maltese dog. The American Maltese Association was established in 1961. Prior to the existence of what we know today as the American Maltese Association, a few Maltese clubs existed. The Maltese Terrier Club of America, which was formally organized in 1906, was the first Maltese dog association established in America. This club eventually became known as the National Maltese Club. The American Kennel Club has records of this club having held its first specialty dog show at the Waldorf Astoria Hotel in New York in 1917. Nearly forty years later there were two Maltese dog clubs in existence: the Maltese Dog Club of America (formerly the National Maltese Club), and the Maltese Dog Fanciers of America. In 1961 the presidents and representatives from these two dog clubs met to form what we know of today as the American Maltese Association.

The American Maltese Association is a good source for those in search of purebred Maltese. There is a breeder referral contact listed on the website for those in the market to buy a Maltese dog. Also, the American Maltese Association operates a national rescue program to relocate temporarily homeless Maltese in foster and permanent homes.

Breed Clubs

The American Kennel Club (AKC), founded in 1884, is the most influential dog club in the United States. The AKC is a "club of clubs," meaning that its members are other kennel clubs, not individual people. The AKC registers purebred dogs, supervises dog shows, and is concerned with all dog-related matters, including public education and legislation. It collects and publishes the official standards for all of its recognized breeds.

The United Kingdom version of the AKC is called the Kennel Club. However, the Kennel Club's members are individual persons. The membership of the Kennel Club is restricted to a maximum of 1,500 UK members in addition to 50 overseas members and a small number of honorary life members. The Kennel Club promotes responsible dog ownership and works on important issues like canine health and welfare.

Chapter

2

CHARACTERISTICS
of the Maltese

W hile the Maltese has gotten the reputation of being a frou-frou dog, don't be fooled. There's steel inside that ball of fluff. Remember that the earliest Maltese were mousers and ratters of renown and it takes a tough dog to square off against a rat. Although he has always been regarded as a status symbol, the real value of the Maltese lies in his ability to be the ultimate companion dog. In fact, the unique charm of the Maltese is that he is all things: tough and tender, powderpuff and powerball. This breed is very loving—and very demanding. He has a loyal heart, but his owner must be worthy of that loyalty.

Let's take a look at some of the important physical characteristics of this stunning breed.

PHYSICAL ATTRIBUTES OF THE MALTESE

The Maltese is a toy dog, but he is anything but a toy. Known for his flowing, pure white coat, gentle but alert facial expression, and overall carriage, this self-composed, self-assured little fellow simply breathes sophistication.

Coat

The compact, square body of the Maltese is covered with a single coat of long, straight, silky, white hair that hangs to the ground when the coat is left unclipped. However, you should know that the gorgeous flowing coat of a Maltese show dog is beyond the reach of most pet owners, as it takes immense labor (including wrapping the coat) to keep it in condition. Most show dogs are kept inside all the time; they're also carried a lot. Most pet owners clip the coat so that it doesn't drag along the ground, picking up anything and everything.

A single coat means that the Maltese does not have the thick, downy undercoat

The gorgeous flowing coat of a Maltese show dog is beyond the reach of most pet owners.

of most other breeds, making him an appealing choice to people with allergies. However, no dog is guaranteed hypoallergenic, and it's not wise to purchase a dog like this in the hope it will be the one breed that won't make you sneeze. It is fair to say that the Maltese is a minimal shedder. The color ranges from a pure white to a white with subtle tones of light-tan, beige, and lemon.

Head

The head of the Maltese is of medium length and in proportion to that of the body. The skull is slightly rounded on the top with plumes of hair streaming down and covering its eyes. Groomers and owners of the Maltese typically tie this hair in knots, up in a bow, or trim it short as to not obstruct the vision of the Maltese. The stop, which is the place where the muzzle meets the nose, is of moderate size. The Maltese has low-set, drop ears, which hang close to the head. They are covered with long white hair as is the rest of the body. The eyes, which should not be set too far apart, are dark and round with black rims. The muzzle is of medium length and in complete proportion to the rest of its head. The Maltese's black nose matches his black-rimmed eyes. Don't be shocked if your Malty's nose goes pale in the winter, a condition called (appropriately enough), "snow nose." Sometimes a little exposure to the sun will return it to his summer color again.

It is equally correct in the Maltese to have the teeth meet in an edge-to-edge "level" bite, or for the upper teeth to slightly overhang the lower teeth in a scissors bite. The neck of the Maltese should promote a high carriage of the head.

Size

The average weight of a Maltese ranges between 4 and 9 pounds (2 and 4 kg), with 6 pounds (3 kg) as the average and often preferred weight. Male Maltese stand between 8 to 10 inches (20 to 25 cm). Maltese females are slightly smaller—they range between 8 to 9 inches (20 to 23 cm). This is a compact dog, and the height from the withers (shoulders) to the ground should equal the length from the withers to the root of the tail.

Body

The Maltese's shoulder blades are sloping, with elbows well knit and held close to the body. ("Well knit" is a doggie conformation term that simply refers to body parts joined by strong muscles.) The back should be level, with rounded ribs. The chest is fairly deep, the loins taut, strong, and just slightly tucked up underneath.

Tail

The Maltese carries his long-plumed tail gracefully over the back, with the tip lying to the side.

Legs

The legs and feet of the Maltese are fine boned. The front legs should be nice and straight, while the rear end is strong, with a moderate bend at the knee and hock, or "heel." You'll notice that a dog's heel is higher off the ground than yours is—dogs run on their toes. The feet of the Maltese are small and round with black toe pads and clear nails. Scraggly hairs grow between the toes, which need to be trimmed.

Gait

The Maltese moves with a jaunty, smooth, flowing gait. Viewed from the side the Maltese gives an impression of rapid movement—as though he is floating. This is in part due to the Maltese's floor-length hair. In the stride, the forelegs reach

Fragile Dogs

Probably the greatest drawback of the Maltese is his fragility. After all, this is a very small dog, no matter how brave. You could do serious harm to your dog by not watching where you're walking! Maltese can also hurt themselves just by jumping off of a chair or sofa. And, of course, a larger dog could easily hurt your Maltese with one well-placed snap. Make no mistake, this is a breed that needs to be carefully supervised at all times.

The Maltese's gentle nature makes him the perfect lap dog.

straight and are free from the shoulders, with elbows close to the body. The hind legs move in a straight line in accordance with the flow of the body. A hind leg bent inwards or outwards is considered a fault.

Temperament

The Maltese is both gentle and fearless, combining the most important qualities of a lap dog with a watchdog. They are super at both jobs! Gentle and affectionate with their owners, and sometimes wary of strangers, these little guys are charming and playful, but strong-willed.

Despite his small size, the Maltese is an excellent watchdog, alerting the household to any suspicious goings on. They are highly intelligent and excellent learners, often excelling at obedience and other doggy accomplishments—if their owners will only give them a chance to be real dogs rather than lap-warmers. The Maltese is capable of great things, if treated correctly—gently without pampering—although I'd be the first one to admit it's hard not to spoil these little charmers.

IS THE MALTESE RIGHT FOR YOU?

So, now that you understand the make-up of the typical Maltese, it's time to decide whether this beautiful little dog is right to join your family. Consider the following questions.

Are You Looking for an Athlete?

If your idea of fun is a day-long hike in the wilderness, battling bitter winds while racing up mountain paths, and swimming powerful rivers, you may need a more primitive breed. The Maltese is a true child of civilization, happiest in your quiet company, and perfectly ready for a long evening by the hearth or dancing in the kitchen. Like all dogs, they do need regular exercise to keep fit, but a daily walk or two will fill their needs. Many seem to get all they need running around the house, although like all sentient beings, they suffer boredom without a change of scenery.

Remember that all dogs need exercise—it's a great way to work off those extra ounces, which are not only damaging to the health but unattractive. A fat Maltese is as close to ugly as a Maltese can get. But walking a Maltese is a real joy. You don't need to gallop along to keep up—and the Maltese's classic good looks will ensure any number of people stopping you to compliment you on your handsome little dog. These frequent stops allow both of you to catch your breath if you need it. Besides, having a dog will get you moving too. Some recent studies have found that would-be dieters are more regular with their exercise and apt to lose weight if they have a dog to walk!

In hot weather, take those walks in the early morning and evening when it's a little cooler. In winter, you may wish to add a snazzy sweater to your dog's wardrobe, or even a pair of booties, particularly if it's bitter cold or the sidewalks are covered with ice-melting chemicals. (It's not silly—the Huskies of the Iditarod wear them). A walk three times a day (15 minutes each time) should suffice.

Do You Have Time to Groom Your Maltese— Every Day?

Like all long-coated dogs, the Maltese needs regular grooming. If you decide to keep the coat in its natural, long state, you will have to comb and brush out your dog every day without fail. If not, the coat will mat hideously and you will have to shave it off, and a shaved Maltese looks very peculiar. However, there is an up side to daily brushing—it enhances the bond between you and your dog. Besides, even

The Importance of Socialization

Maltese are sweet tempered by nature. A dog who is snappish or aggressive may not have been properly socialized with strangers or other dogs. Unfortunately, in the past many breeders allowed Maltese to get away with being ill-natured, but enlightened breeders today have been working diligently to remove inherited aggressive tendencies from the breed. They also take steps to socialize their puppies early. A Maltese may never be overjoyed to meet strangers (although many are), but they should never be permitted to become little tyrants over the household. Princes and princesses, maybe.

Even if your Maltese doesn't have a show coat, you'll still have to groom him daily.

though the Maltese needs regular grooming, he is such a small dog that if you attend to him every day, it shouldn't take more than ten minutes. The Maltese has a "single coat" without the thick downy undercoat that most other breeds have (and which flies all over the house).

Some people who suffer from pet allergies often will not have a reaction to a Maltese. In this respect, the Maltese is a wonderful option for someone who thought they could never own a dog due to their allergies. However, this is not guaranteed. If you are allergic to dogs, don't assume that a Maltese is the answer to your health problems. At the very least arrange to spend some time with one before you plunge into ownership. It would be tragic indeed to have to give him away after you have fallen in love.

You can elect to keep the coat clipped, which is easier to care for, but in that case, your Maltese will lack the unique characteristic of the breed. Of course his personality will be unchanged no matter what his coat looks like.

Can You Shower Your Maltese With Attention?

The Maltese was bred as a companion dog and is very dependent upon your company. The Maltese is known for bonding to his owner and will want to be in your presence at all times, even times when it might be inconvenient for you. Maltese left alone for long hours every day are subject to separation anxiety, which produces a host of problems for the owner or the neighbors, including incessant barking, house soiling, and destruction. If you are away from home for many hours a day, consider a different breed of dog, or perhaps a self-sufficient cat. The Maltese takes great pleasure in sharing all the moments of your life, and people who prefer an independent dog should look elsewhere. Some people choose to hire a mid-day dog walker to exercise and entertain their Maltese, while others send their little friend to a doggy day care center.

Do You Have Children?

A Maltese can fit perfectly into any family, so long as the parents supervise interactions between toddlers and the dog. Because of their small size, Maltese they can be easily injured, and because they are sensitive beings, they may snap or bite if teased. Maltese are not dogs who simply hang around waiting to be mistreated. They are wonderful with gentle, older children, enjoy playing games with them, and will even attempt to protect them from perceived dangers. Older folks, disabled people and apartment dwellers are especially great prospective owners for the breed.

If you have toddlers, it is your responsibility to always supervise when they are with a dog. Never allow a small child to pick the Maltese up (she may drop him). Instead, hold the dog yourself and show the child how to stroke him gently.

Do You Want a Loyal Companion?

If this is the case, then you are in luck. The Maltese is one of the most loyal of the toy breeds, affectionate, cheerful and delighted to be in your company at home or on the road. The one place your Maltese does not belong is alone in the backyard for extended periods of time. (For a Maltese, an extended period of time might be five minutes.) These are primarily indoor dogs, and when left alone outside they get (1) very dirty, (2) into trouble, (3) stolen. You don't want any of those things to happen. Your Maltese is your companion and pet, not a moving lawn ornament.

I cannot stress enough how much the Maltese requires in human companionship. He'll pay you back with unconditional love, though, so it's a great bargain. Maltese are extremely fond of being petted—and that's good news for you too! Many studies have shown that cuddling and stroking your pet is good for your health; it makes you more relaxed and can even lower your heart rate and blood pressure. You can also talk to your Maltese; he may not answer you but he'll

"Teacup" Maltys

Run like mad if your hear a breeder refer to his or her dogs as "teacup." There is no such category; it's a slang term used by people who are trying to convince an unwary buyer that smaller is better. The ideal adult Maltese is no smaller than 4 pounds (2 kg).

enjoy the sound of your voice! He won't argue, interrupt, or reveal your secrets. And it's sort of amazing how you can find the answer to your own problems once you tell them to your dog.

Can You Handle a Smarty-Pants?

The Maltese is an extremely intelligent breed. On the whole, like the rest of the toy breeds, they tend to have housetraining problems, but patience and consistency on your part can help overcome this issue. Largely, this is because they have small bladders, not because of any willfulness or utter disregard for your carpet.

When it comes to learning commands and tricks they are extremely quick to learn. Because of their intelligence they make excellent show dogs and have been known to perform well in obedience and performance events, including agility. The Maltese is a brilliant dog and will show his intelligence if you are diligent with his training and use the power of positive reinforcement to teach him.

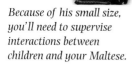

Because of his small size, you'll need to supervise interactions between children and your Maltese.

Do You Need a Watch Dog?

Despite his small size, the Maltese is an excellent guardian of house and home. This breed is known to be protective and territorial of his home. Maltese are small dogs, but that does not necessarily mean that they won't defend their territory. His acute hearing alerts him to intruders, burglars, the mail carrier, relatives, or anyone else knocking at the door—and he'll be sure to alert you. The bark of the Maltese is rather high pitched, as are most barks of small breed dogs. This barking alone may be enough to scare off an unsuspecting intruder. However, if you are specifically looking for a guard-rather than a watchdog, a Maltese might not be the best breed for you. After all, a hairy 6 pound (3 kg) toy breed doesn't seem quite as menacing as a large German Shepherd Dog or Doberman Pinscher.

Do You Live in the City or Country?

If you live in an urban environment, in a condominium or apartment, Maltese are a wonderful choice, for they are natural city-slickers. Maltese do well in small living quarters and can be quite happy in an apartment. They are healthy and happy with a walk or two a day and a few visits outside to relieve themselves. Just keep in mind that this breed loves the outdoors, so make sure that you expose your dog to the outside at least a few times a day with short walks or one long walk. Walking should be a year round staple for your Maltese; he doesn't want to stare at four walls all day any more than you do.

The Maltese can also adjust to country living, as long as you don't expect him to herd the sheep or sleep under the front porch. They love romps in the grass and an occasional stroll down the back forty, although you might have to carry him back up. But that's okay—they don't weigh much.

Do You Have Other Pets?

Opinions differ as to how well the Maltese will get along with other pets, so I suspect it's largely an individual matter. Certainly a Maltese may feel overwhelmed by a Rottweiler, and it may not be a good idea to get one as a companion to a

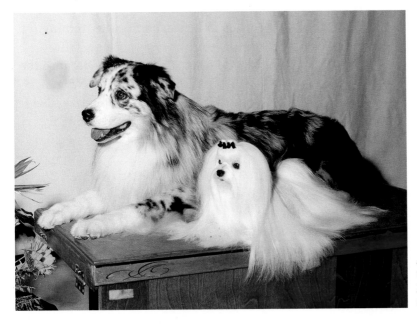

As long as both dogs are well-socialized, some Maltese can get along well with bigger dogs.

Barking Problems

Your Maltese's barking can easily be considered a nuisance if he constantly barks at people like the letter carrier or friends who come to visit. If this is the case, you'll need to search out methods of training your Maltese to not bark, or hire a professional trainer or behaviorist to help. See Chapter 6 to learn more about handling behavioral problems.

predatory dog like a Greyhound; this is even more true if the Maltese is a puppy, whose tiny yip may sound unnervingly like a mouse squeaking. However, I have known a Maltese who got along perfectly well with a Mastiff. Some Maltese seem to not notice their own size, and tend to be fearless when it comes to approaching or playing with larger dogs. Do be careful, as some larger dogs may not return the affection. When it comes to a large dog living with a Maltese, you might want to consider feeding them in separate rooms, as fights can occur between the best of canine friends when food is involved.

Maltese can get along well with cats in the household. However, be cautious because a cat may choose to use her claws in play, which can cause severe damage to the eyes of a tiny Maltese. Older cats sometimes need to be watched closely with a new Maltese puppy, as they might appear to be prey (much like a small rodent). As the Maltese matures and understands how to approach the cat this problem should be alleviated.

On the whole, the Maltese is compatible with other pets, but always take precautions when introducing a new dog, as your Maltese is a fragile and gentle little being.

Are You Willing to Crate Train?

The Maltese is a breed that adapts well to crate training. Regardless of whether or not you live in an urban or rural environment you should crate train your Maltese. Because the Maltese is such a small dog, he will find comfort having a small space all of his own in the larger-than-life human-sized living space. If you are interested in crate training your Maltese you'll find more information in Chapter 6.

Can You Make a Fifteen-Year Commitment?

The Maltese lives on average about 13 to 16 years. Some, however, have lived as long as 19 years or more. Their life span will naturally increase if they are treated well by their owners, fed a healthy diet, given adequate amounts of exercise throughout their life, and have regular visits to the veterinarian. They tend to remain playful and sprightly throughout the majority of their life, even in old age. (I knew

Maltese have expressive faces.

one who got his first obedience degree at age 12!)

Compared to some other breeds, Maltese suffer from few genetic disorders, and are generally quite healthy. (I'll talk more about health problems in Chapter 8.)

Are You Planning on Breeding Your Maltese?

Please do not purchase a Maltese with the intention of breeding—leave that to experienced and knowledgeable breeders. Many people, when they first become aware of this lovely breed, soon come to the conclusion that it would be a wonderful idea to buy a female puppy and raise a litter from her in the future. Some people believe breeding is a great way to make a quick profit, but be aware—it is nearly impossible to make money ethically breeding dogs. Good breeders do not breed dogs to make a profit; they breed dogs for the love of the breed.

Breeding is hard, time-consuming, and requires knowledge of genetics. Also, there are many things that can go wrong during whelping, and the complications can be heartbreaking.

You need only to visit a local animal shelter to view the

problem of pet overpopulation and over-breeding firsthand. Maltese are a lovely elegant breed and are rarely seen in shelter populations. This is because dedicated breeders who know and understand the breed standard are carefully and ethically breeding and placing their dogs.

Can You Read Maltese?

While people talk with words, (and dogs vocalize as well) Maltese use their expressive bodies to tell us many things. Here's a general guide to reading your Malty:

- **Standing "tall"**: Maltese who stand tall and proud are exhibiting confidence.
- **Standing tiptoe**: Confidence has edged over into dominance and potential aggression.
- **Rolling over**: This is submissive behavior. By being "vulnerable" they are also asking you (even if only in play) to have mercy on them.
- **Leaning against you**: Shows a proprietary affection.
- **Pawing**: He wants something.
- **Bowing**: Play-soliciting behavior; he wants to romp.

Acquiring a dog comes with many responsibilites.

- **Raised hackles**: Fear or hostility.
- **"Humping" human legs**: If he's not sterilized and doing this behavior, he's probably trying to assert his authority over you; this behavior may also be a sign of a hormonal health problem.

THE MALTESE: A SYMBOL OF STATUS

Since his origins, the Maltese has been a symbol of status. He has been seated in the lap of luxury as a favorite of royalty, companion to the women in the harems of ancient Egypt, and held as an "accessory" in the arms of the elite during the eras of the Roman and Greek Empires. With dog shows on the rise in the late 1800s, the Maltese gained in popularity with dog fanciers captivated by his winning attitude. Today, the Maltese is still seen as a symbol of the elite.

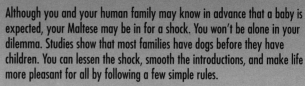

However, acquiring a Maltese because of the breed's popularity or to display an elevated social standing is absolutely the wrong reason to become an owner of this dog. You should venture into Maltese ownership with the intent of gaining a companion in life, not a status symbol. Realize that with acquiring a dog comes many responsibilities. Your Maltese will be dependent on you for his entire life. You'll need to be ready and willing to provide food, shelter, and medical care for your dog. Of course, the rewards are immense, for in return you will receive complete loyalty and unconditional love from your Maltese. Just make sure you are getting him for all the right reasons.

Dogs and Babies

Although you and your human family may know in advance that a baby is expected, your Maltese may be in for a shock. You won't be alone in your dilemma. Studies show that most families have dogs before they have children. You can lessen the shock, smooth the introductions, and make life more pleasant for all by following a few simple rules.

- Clue the dog into the fact that things are changing. (He may sense it anyway.) Let him watch you prepare the nursery and share in the excitement. Make sure that everything he associates with the coming change is positive. Be happy and give him lots of treats while doing "baby things."

- Let him meet other babies—on a leash, of course. Let him get used to the sight, sound, and smell of them.

- Make sure that he enters the baby's room only when invited.

- Practice carrying a large doll around the house.

- When the baby comes home, have the dog stay somewhere else, even for a few hours. When he arrives home, the baby is a "done deal"— already at home. This will encourage your Maltese to accept him.

- Act positively with your Maltese in the presence of the baby. That way he'll associate the child with positive things.

Chapter

3

PREPARING
for Your Maltese

I ncredible as it may seem, not everyone should own a dog, let alone a super dog like a Maltese. Adding a Malty to your family is like acquiring a new child. He is a friend who will be with you as long as he lives, which will be well into his teens. If you bought this book before you acquired your Maltese, you've already done one thing right: you've prepared.

BEFORE YOU TAKE THE PLUNGE

Before you take the plunge, take this test to see whether or not getting a dog is right for you and your family. The purpose of these questions is not to scare you, but to help you decide how well a dog would fit into your life right now.

Can You Afford a Dog?

Sorry to be blunt, but this is something that you need to assess realistically. Dogs are not cheap. Whether you spend a thousand dollars on a top show prospect or get one free from your brother-in-law, canine costs add up fast, especially in the first year. In fact, the initial cost of the dog is the smallest expense. You'll need to buy dog supplies like a crate, bed, leashes, and neckwear. High-quality dog food isn't cheap, and neither are vet bills. Your dog will need immunizations and regular veterinary care, and there's no guarantee that he won't ever get sick or have an accident.

You'll be the center of your Malty's life, so make sure you have enough time to spend with him.

Since every dog improves with obedience training, you should sign up for a class. If you're a first time dog owner, you'll learn more than the dog will. These classes are a terrific investment, but they're not cheap.

If you plan on taking a vacation, and can't take your Malty, you'll have to consider boarding costs. (Maltese do like to go on vacation, though. They prefer five-star hotels, but they'll endure anything just to be with you.) All in all, your first year's Maltese expenses, including regular vet bills and high quality dog food, can run into thousands of dollars. This figure doesn't include extras like boarding fees or special expenses like fencing.

How Much Time Do You Have to Spend With a Dog ?

Your dog doesn't stand quietly in the corner when you don't need him. You're the center of his life, and he requires your loving, regular attention. Although dogs can sleep an amazing fourteen hours a day, that leaves ten hours when they're wide awake, waiting for something to happen and someone to play with them. Some people feel that just being home around the dog is enough, but dogs thrive on personalized attention. Human beings developed dogs as companion animals, and

companionship is what they need. Sadly, some people lavish attention on their young dogs, and conveniently forget about them as they grow older and less "cute." Dogs don't understand this attitude.

Good dog ownership means devoting a fair-sized chunk of your day to feeding, exercising, playing with, grooming, and picking up after your dog. And besides those "fun" things, you'll need time to go to the vet, the pet supply store, the puppy sitter, and the dog trainer. One of the reasons that modern dogs have acquired so many behavioral problems is that they simply don't get enough company. They aren't being bad—they are just lonely and bored. And when dogs get lonely, they can become destructive and neurotic.

What is your career outlook? Do you have a job that may require you to move? What are your plans for your dog in that case? Unless you are determined to keep a dog with you as a permanent part of your family no matter what, it's best not to get a dog at all.

Does Everyone in Your Family Really Want a Dog?

Make sure everyone in the family truly wants a dog, and that the dog they want is a Maltese. It always amazes me how many people get the Maltese of their dreams, and bring it home, only to discover that everyone else in the house wanted a Great Dane—or a hamster. Many dogs end up in shelters or with a rescue organization because they were purchased over the objections of one family member, who then gets saddled with walking, feeding, and cleaning up after the

Kids and Responsibility

Although children promise to be responsible for the dog, they have a habit of getting tired of or forgetting their obligations from time to time. If this happens, the job falls to you. It's not fair to anyone to get a dog in order to "teach responsibility" to a child. You're the parent. If you have to be at work, away from home ten hours a day, you may have to re-think your plan to get a dog.

unwanted pet. Resentment builds, and the dog may suffer as a result. So before you actually go out and choose a Malty, get everyone's whole-hearted approval.

Are You Allowed to Have a Dog?

Be sure you verify (don't just assume) that your real estate covenant or rental agreement allows dogs. Get permission in writing. Don't take a chance on the welfare of your Maltese by trying to sneak him in, hoping you won't get caught. Sooner or later he will be found out, and you'll be in the uncomfortable position of having to decide between your dog and your home.

Are You Prepared for a Maltese?

Maltese are different. If your only canine experience has been with a Labrador Retriever or German Shepherd Dog, you may be in for a shock. While the Maltese wishes to make you happy, he is not a "push button" obedience dog. You must be prepared to meet a Maltese on his own terms (which often includes bribery).

WHERE TO START

Okay, okay. You pass! You'll change jobs, sell your stock, and remodel the house just to get that Maltese. You're even willing to housetrain one. You've waited long enough and are ready to start looking. First, you'll have to decide if a puppy or adult is right for you, if you'd rather have a male or female, and whether or not you are looking for a show dog or a pet.

Puppy or Adult?

Will a puppy or adult Maltese best suit your lifestyle? Both of these options have pros and cons.

Puppies

Puppies are cute, cuddly, and oh so hard to resist. One look at an adorable little Maltese puppy is sure to melt your heart. Aside from the "cute factor," when you purchase a puppy you are more or less working with a blank slate. As long as you've chosen a breeder who cares about temperament, you are more likely to be able to train and instill your Maltese with all of the values, tricks and behavior you want him to have.

On the other hand, buying a puppy may not be the best

option for you. A puppy, although adorable, comes with a huge time and money commitment, including providing him with all of his shots, a series of veterinary visits, housetraining, obedience, and socialization. Are you ready to get up several times a night, in all types of weather, to take your puppy out for those potty breaks he's going to need? Are you willing to go through the puppy teething stage, where he'll want to chew on his bed, toys, your furniture, Aunt Edna's antique rug, and anything else he can get his paws on? Are you willing to constantly supervise him, and give him all the proper socialization he needs? If after thinking about these questions the answer is yes, than a puppy may be right for you.

If your heart is set on a puppy, you'll probably end up acquiring him at anywhere from 8 to 12 weeks old (depending on the breeder). Younger puppies may not be sufficiently socialized with other dogs (something they learn in the litter), while older ones, if they have not had intensive interaction with people, may need more socialization. (The critical canine/human socialization period is from the third through the sixteenth week. If puppies are not adequately socialized to humans during this period, they probably never will be.) Having said that, I should add that I have raised puppies who have left the litter at various ages. I have also adopted many adult dogs. They all turned out pretty well.

Puppies are so cute and hard to resist!

The Maltese has been stigmatized as difficult to housetrain, as are a majority of the toy breeds. However, if you are diligent and structured with your housetraining, you should not have a problem with your Maltese. See Chapter 6 for more information on housetraining.

Adults

If you've thought about the time and commitment needed to train a puppy and are thinking it may be too much, you may choose to rescue an adult Maltese. There are many positive aspects to adopting an older dog. Most likely an adult dog has already been neutered or spayed; he'll have finished what can be a costly series of vet visits and vaccinations that happen in the first year of life; and he is more likely to be housetrained or even obedience trained. (The process of training a puppy can take anywhere from six months to a year).

Some rescue adult dogs do have behavior problems, but my experience is that nothing is more trouble than a puppy. (They are cute, though….)

Show or Pet?

Not all Maltese, even from a show breeder, are "show quality." This doesn't necessarily mean the dog is a bad dog; it simply means that he lacks one or more qualities that could make him a champion in the show ring. Many of these "faults" are extremely minor: a too short neck, tan or lemon color on the ears, or other small imperfections may deny a dog a championship, but have absolutely no effect on the dog's health or beauty. Unless you specifically tell the breeder that you are interested in showing dogs, you will be sold a pet-quality dog. Some breeders charge less for pet quality dogs; others don't.

Male or Female?

Or, as we say in the dog world, dog or bitch? This is a matter of personal preference. Males and females don't differ markedly in temperament, although some people say that females are more affectionate, while others believe they are more "demanding." Some claim males have a more consistent temperament. Others say males tend to be more dominant. Males do tend to be slightly larger, but the difference is too small to worry about.

Whatever sex you choose, remember to spay or neuter your pet Maltese unless you are planning on showing the dog. Unaltered animals roam, mark, come into heat, fight with other dogs, and make general nuisances of themselves. Altered dogs suffer fewer health problems, are less destructive, less aggressive, and tend to be happier at home.

WHERE TO FIND THE MALTESE OF YOUR DREAMS

Once you have decided on a Maltese puppy or adult, a male or female, show or pet quality, you'll need to decide exactly where to find the Maltese of your dreams. There are many options available: breeders, pet stores, rescues and (sometimes) shelters. It's important to do your research in order to find a healthy dog who is right for you.

Breeders

If you have decided on getting your Maltese through a breeder, you must be diligent about finding a reputable one. There are a select few Maltese breeders, and finding the right one for you will take some time and a bit of research.

Where to Find a Breeder

The easiest way to find a good breeder, if you don't have personal contacts, is to check out the American Kennel Club (AKC) website (www.akc.org). This site will provide you with the names and addresses of Maltese clubs near you. (They also post rescue sites, listed in the appendix of this book.) When it comes to finding a specific breeder, the AKC suggests that you refer to the American Maltese Association (www.americanmaltese.org). The American Maltese Association is the nationally recognized parent breed club of the AKC, and has breeder lists that are searchable by state on their website. If you find your breeder through the American Maltese Association it is likely that you are dealing with a reliable source.

You can also call a nearby kennel club and ask for a list of reputable breeders in your area—the club will be thrilled to comply with your request. They know that wise buyers benefit the breed as a whole. If possible, join a local Maltese club before you even get your dog. What better way to learn about the breed and meet fellow Maltese enthusiasts? (If you get chummy enough with one of them,

"Hobby" Breeders

Curiously enough, the best choice of breeder is the so-called "hobby breeder." A hobby breeder is no rank amateur, but someone who breeds for the love of the breed, rather than for financial gain. She doesn't depend on selling Maltese for a living. She probably takes her dogs to shows because she is proud of them and of her role in producing them. She enjoys breeding a litter occasionally, and is interested in improving her line of Maltese. Selling to the highest bidder isn't on her list of things-to-do today. You won't see dozens and dozens of dogs locked up in a pen in the back yard. A good hobby breeder has made her well-socialized dogs part of her own family, and her pups will easily become part of yours.

Good breeders care about the health and genetics of their puppies.

she might go along to help you find the perfect puppy or older dog.)

Another place to look for a breeder is to attend a few dog shows. Dogs shows are held throughout the year, and you can find one near you by checking the AKC's website. The world of dog shows can be pretty mysterious to the novice, but go anyway. It'll give you an idea what a nice Maltese should look like (if you can see anything under the hair). This is especially important if you think you might like to show your dog some day.

If you find a Maltese you think is particularly handsome, ask his handler or breeder if there's an upcoming litter or dogs from related lines. Don't do this right before a class, however, since people tend to be a little tense then. Approach the person after the classes have been judged. I always start with a compliment to the dog in question. Most breeders are happy to talk with serious students of the breed. If you encounter someone who is rude, chalk it up to "bad breeding" and talk to a more amenable person.

Good breeders usually have a line of people waiting to buy puppies, so be prepared to wait. Maltese litters are often quite small, with a range of 2 to 4 puppies per litter. An ethical breeder will not constantly have Maltese puppies for sale—they are more concerned with the health of the mother than having puppies to sell.

Visiting the Breeder

When you make contact with a good breeder, make a list of

questions, and be prepared to answer a few questions as well. Responsible breeders have more potential buyers than they have puppies, and breeders have high standards for their litters. Don't be offended if the breeder asks you "nosy" questions about your house, yard, fencing, working hours, dog-owning expertise, and planned sleeping arrangements for the puppy. A good breeder wants the best for her dogs, and she wants to make sure you and the puppy will be a good match. It's a bad sign if the breeder seems more interested in your pocketbook than in the way you interact with her dogs. Be suspicious of breeders who seem too anxious to sell their puppies, who assert that all their dogs are show quality, or who seem reluctant to provide verifiable health information.

Questions you need to ask the breeder include how long she has been breeding dogs, and what titles they have won. Although every breeder has to begin at some point, inexperienced buyers are best matched with experienced breeders. Ask the breeder how often she breeds—breeders with large numbers of litters over a short period are suspect. One question I have used to sort out good breeders from bad ones is to ask: "What are the goals of your breeding program?" If the breeder stares at you blankly, you may want to reconsider buying a dog from her. A responsible breeder, however, once you broach this topic, will not stop talking about it.

Even if you don't know a lot about dogs or dog breeding, you should be able to spot a top-notch facility. A good breeder will have a clean, sheltered facility, preferably indoors. When you visit, pay close attention to the mother dog, especially her temperament. Temperament is largely inherited. If the mother is merry, outgoing, and amiable, it's likely the puppies will grow up to be the same way. The temperament of the stud dog is also important, although the dad may not be on hand for viewing. Many high-quality dogs are bred from parents who happen not to live together. (Family values in Maltese aren't all that they might be.) Seeing a photo or videotape of the dad may have to suffice. Keep in mind that simply having both parents on the premises is no guarantee of quality.

Notice how the breeder interacts with her Maltese. They should seem happy, cheerful and

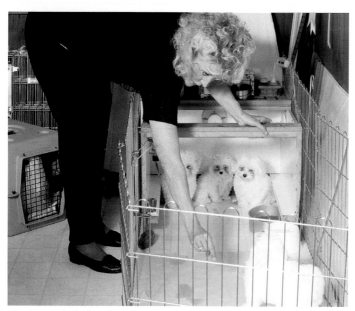

The breeder's facility should be clean and well kept.

comfortable around her. If her dogs seem shy, frightened, or reluctant to come close, reconsider.

A good breeder can provide references from previous customers. It's a good idea to call these folks, and ask questions about the health and temperament of the Maltese they purchased. A breeder who's unwilling to supply references may have something to hide. A good breeder will also agree to take the dog back at any time if you can no longer keep him. A good breeder is honest about the shortcomings as well as the glories of the Maltese. No breed is perfect, and each comes with its own potential health problems.

Selecting Your Special Puppy

When you visit the breeder to select your puppy, you'll want a friendly and outgoing dog, not one who is shy or aggressive. Your best pet is usually to pick a "middle-of-the road" puppy, who neither hangs back nor charges forward. Watch the puppies play together. Compare how the puppy you like acts towards his littermates. Is he much more or a great deal less active than the others? Some very forward or "pushy" puppies may be on their way to alpha or "top dog" status. Alpha puppies can turn into very dominant dogs, and are best bought by people who are experienced in dealing with them. Breeders often know which of the puppies are their "alpha" dogs. In addition, highly excitable puppies usually turn into highly excitable dogs, and may end up with more behavioral problems than the laid-back type.

Thus, it may be best to select a more submissive (but not shy) puppy for your home, especially if you are a first-time dog owner, or if you have young children. On the other hand, if you are looking for a show dog, a high-spirited, independent alpha may be just the ticket. Ask the breeder for help. Sometimes, prospective owners just fall in love with a certain puppy without listening to what the breeder has to say about his personality. Pay attention and choose with your head as well as your heart.

You should be able to touch your prospective puppy all over without getting a frightened or hostile response. Pick up the puppy of your choice. (He should feel heavier than you thought!) He should show no fear of you or of the breeder. A good puppy is friendly and happy to be near you, although he may squirm a little (that's in the nature of puppies, after all). However, if you are playing gently with the puppy, and he doesn't relax after half an hour, he may be genetically hyperactive. See how eagerly the puppy will follow you, and how responsive he seems to your words and voice. Happy-to-follow-along puppies will be easier to train later.

Healthy puppies are plump, but not pot-bellied. (A distended belly could signify parasites.) Their ears, skin, and gums should be pink, not red or pale. They should move well even at eight weeks, and carry their tails high. They should be clean and sweet smelling. The eyes and ears should be discharge-free, and the feces should be well formed.

When you have selected your puppy, make sure that the breeder contract allows you to take him to your veterinarian for a thorough checkup before the purchase is complete.

Paperwork

It is important that you are meticulous regarding the paperwork that comes with purchasing your puppy. Make sure that the sale is in writing. The contract should include details regarding any fees, spay-neuter agreements, health guarantees, terms of co-ownership, restrictions on breeding, and living arrangements. In addition, the contract should include terms of how to proceed if the dog, despite your best efforts and intentions, simply does not work with your lifestyle or family. If your breeder is responsible, she will insist, in writing, that the Maltese be returned to her rather than be put up for

Get the Family Involved

When visiting the breeder to select your puppy, bring along the whole family. Everyone should have some input into choosing the family dog. Steel yourself; buy with your head as well as your heart. To prevent impulse buying, don't bring your checkbook on the first visit. One look in those eyes and it's all over. Make yourself go home, re-think your decision, and if you're sure, then go back and bring home (or reserve) your puppy. Of course, if you've traveled a long way to see this litter, you have so much invested that you'll have a hard time turning it down. Before you make any long-distance plans, ask for photos.

Rescue and adoption organizations will ask you plenty of questions before you adopt.

adoption or given to a shelter.

In addition to a contract, you will need to fill out the appropriate paperwork for your kennel club of choice. Registering your Maltese with a national club like the American Kennel Club, United Kennel Club, or Kennel Club of England, is beneficial to you as a dog owner on several levels. A registered dog can participate in any of the events in which the Maltese breed is qualified to participate, including dog shows. Many clubs offer special services like health insurance, informative magazines, and other helpful information when you register.

The Adoption Option

There are national rescue organizations dedicated to rescuing purebred dogs who have been lost, abandoned, or surrendered due to the death or illness of their owners. There are many great reasons to rescue a dog instead of buying a new puppy. Most rescued dogs have already been spayed or neutered, saving you the cost. Also, most rescue groups screen the dogs for health and temperament problems. Rescue is not only an excellent source to acquire a purebred Maltese; it's an excellent way to save the life of a dog in need.

Rescue may also have a downside. If you have your heart set on a Maltese puppy, it's not very likely you'll be able to find one in rescue. Also, many times you may not be able to find out much about a dog's past history, or even why he was given up. Some rescued dogs can come with behavior problems, so it's best to deal with a rescue that has been temperament tested.

If you decide that an adult Maltese suits your lifestyle better than a Maltese puppy, then rescue may be for you. A great place to start is an organization like the American Maltese Association's Rescue Program. Programs like this offer temporary foster homes for abused, sick, displaced, or homeless Maltese until a permanent home can be found for them. After you contact the rescue program, you will be asked many questions regarding your suitability for Maltese ownership. Expect to answer questions like:

Good to Know

Don't let the breeder tell you that she will send you the papers later. You are entitled to them immediately.

- Do you rent or own your home?
- Do you have a fenced yard? Are there any children in the house? If so, what are their ages?
- Do you own any other pets?
- Have you ever owned a dog? A Maltese?
- Do you have a regular veterinarian?
- Do you understand the grooming needs of this breed?
- Where will the dog spend his day?
- How many hours will the dog be alone each day?

The rescue group may also ask to inspect your home, and require you to sign a statement that if you can no longer care for the dog, he must be returned to rescue.

Just as the rescue group will ask you questions, you need to be diligent in asking some of your own. Ask the person who is handling the rescue or adoption for information on the dog's health, temperament, behavior, and history. Not every dog might have a complete history, so be careful if there is not much background information on the dog. And, as with a breeder, a proper paper trail should follow the process of adopting and rescuing.

Pet Stores

Some people decide to buy a Maltese from a pet store. Pet stores can be a convenient option, and usually offer a wide selection of puppies. The dogs in a pet store are most often well cared for by the staff—fed nutritious food, provided with toys, and kept clean. It's hard to resist them, especially when the store employee offers to let you play with those tiny little guys. It is important to remember that a dog's health is largely dependent on his genetics and the quality of his early care. This is why a responsible pet store should be able to provide you with all the details of your Maltese's breeding and history. Pet store employees should also be knowledgeable about dogs in general and the breeds they sell in particular.

If you decide to purchase a Maltese from a pet store, check the dog for any signs of poor health. A few signs of illness are nasal discharge, watery eyes, and diarrhea. A store should not be selling a dog experiencing any of these symptoms. Even if the puppy seems healthy, be sure to have him checked by your veterinarian as soon as possible. Many health guarantees offered by pet stores are contingent upon a veterinary examination within just days of the sale.

How to Register Your Maltese with the AKC or KC

To register with the AKC, your breeder will have to fill out part of the AKC's registration application. The breeder needs to supply both the dam's and sire's registration numbers, as well as your puppy's number. You complete the application with your name and address, along with the name you have chosen for your puppy. Many breeders require that their kennel name precede the puppy's name—if you bought your Maltese from a kennel called Rosebriar, and you want to name your puppy Princess Matilda, her full registered name would be Rosebriar's Princess Matilda. Of course, yelling "Rosebriar's Princess Matilda, come back here with that shoe!" is quite a mouthful, so you are free to nickname your Maltese anything you want! There is a nonrefundable application fee when you register with the AKC. Check out www.akc.org for more information.

Registering with the Kennel Club in England is the responsibility of the breeder. The breeder will name the puppies, then provide you with a registration certificate for the puppy, which includes a section for the transfer of ownership. After the sale, this section gets sent back to the KC.

Questions to Ask Before Purchasing a Pet Store Puppy

1. *What kind of guarantee do you offer?*

If the store only guarantees the puppy for a few hours or days but offers no compensation for future problems such as genetic diseases, you must be aware that you will be on your own to deal with these problems. The store should be reasonably responsible for ensuring you receive a healthy puppy.

2. *How old was the puppy when he arrived in the store?*

Puppies taken away from their mother and littermates before eight weeks of age are at a great developmental disadvantage. Puppies learn a lot about social interaction from their mother and littermates, and getting shipped across the country in a crate is no way to begin life as a six-week-old puppy. Those taken away too young and exposed to these frightening experiences often develop fearful or aggressive behaviors later in life. The best-case scenario is one in which the puppy was hand delivered by a breeder to a pet store after eight weeks of age.

3. *Can I see the vaccination and worming record?*

Puppies should have had at least one and preferably two sets of complete vaccinations and a worming by eight weeks (this can also depend on the breed). The pet store should have complete documentation of these and any other veterinary care the dogs have received.

4. *Is the puppy registered?*

This is actually a tricky question. Registration is no guarantee of quality, and some registries will register any dog without proof of a pedigree (a written record of a dog's lineage). Dogs who are registered with the American Kennel Club (AKC) or Kennel Club (KC) may be more likely to come from breeders who are following certain standards, but it's not a guarantee. And some small local breeders may provide puppies to pet stores who are unregistered but that could make healthy, fine pets. Yes, it's confusing, but ask anyway, to get the employees talking about the dog, the breeder, and the origin. The more questions you ask about the store's source for puppies, the more you might be able to find out about the breeder's priorities and history.

PREPARING FOR YOUR MALTESE

It is wise to prepare yourself well before the arrival of your new Maltese. You'll want to make your puppy's transition as smooth as possible. Buy all of your dog's supplies weeks in advance (more on exactly what you'll need later in this chapter). You should have enough money budgeted to cover the costs associated with Maltese ownership, such as veterinary bills, grooming, food, and training. If you work during the day make sure that you have looked into doggie daycare options or hired a dog walker. Due to the Maltese's high maintenance coat, you should have a groomer picked out. And don't wait to find a good veterinarian until the last minute.

If you are incorporating your new Maltese into a family, make sure that everyone is prepared and ready for the new addition. Have a family meeting and assign family members different tasks associated with your new dog: feeding, walking, brushing, and cleaning up after him. You might even

The Benefits of ILP

If you are rescuing a Maltese who does not come with papers your dog can still be eligible to participate in American Kennel Club events. The AKC has an Indefinite Listing Privilege (ILP) program that is designed to allow dogs to participate in AKC Companion and Performance Events. By applying for an Indefinite Listing Privilege Number, your Maltese can participate in:

- Agility Trials
- Junior Showmanship
- Obedience Trials
- Rally Trials
- Tracking Tests

Block access to any house or garden plants that may be toxic to your Maltese.

want to post the schedules so that everyone knows their responsibilities, and the dog won't suffer due to a misunderstanding.

Puppy Proofing

Puppies, like little children, get in to everything and anything. Your Maltese will be extremely curious while adjusting to his new surroundings, and some of what he may get into can be hazardous to his health. You can make life safer for your puppy (and your furniture!) by getting rid of potential hazards ahead of time.

Inside the Home

Move breakables and anything that can be chewed out of reach. Hide electrical cords to make them inaccessible to curious paws and noses. Block off any area of the house that you want off-limits to your dog—you might want to install a baby gate or keep the doors to those rooms closed to keep your Maltese out of trouble. If you're in the habit of leaving the lid up on the toilet, start closing it. Put your shoes away in your closet. Make sure you thoroughly clean and pick up any small items that your Maltese could possibly chew on and swallow. This includes making sure that neglected corners of the house are clean, the space under your bed is not harboring any dangerous objects, and small items under tables are picked up.

Dangerous Plants

Block access to any house or garden plants that may be toxic to dogs. Check the ASPCA Animal Poison Control Center or the American Veterinary Medical Association website for a list of common plants that can be dangerous to pets.

As if poisonous plants aren't enough to worry about, many harmless plants are sprayed with insecticides or treated with fertilizers. These products may mask or alter the adverse clinical signs observed in dogs. Even a normally non-toxic plant can cause physical irritation to the gastrointestinal system and subsequent mild stomach upset if it has been sprayed.

Outside the House

It is just as important to puppy proof your yard as it is your home. If your yard is fenced, check the boundaries and gates for openings that could be potential escape routes for your little guy. Like many dogs, Maltese have a tendency to dig, so keep an eye on him when you are outside to make sure he's not working on an escape tunnel worthy of *Hogan's Heroes*. If your yard is not fenced, you might want to consider putting in a dog run. An unfenced yard means your Maltese should be on his leash when taken outdoors.

And while the Maltese is the last breed of dog that should be wandering around your garage, everyone should be aware of the dangers of antifreeze. This tasty substance is extremely toxic, even in small amounts. Although new, less toxic kinds of antifreeze based on propylene glycol are now on the market, many people continue to use those in which the active ingredient is ethylene glycol. This chemical depresses the central nervous system and enters the cerebrospinal fluid, making the dog act as if he is drunk. Unfortunately, the symptoms may not appear until 12 or more hours later (a day and a half in some cases). Untreated it is almost always fatal, as it does irreparable damage to the kidneys. However, if caught early enough, there is an antidote that can help.

For some reason this stuff tastes good to dogs, and they eat it readily. A tablespoon can kill a small dog like your Maltese. Keep your dog away from your garage, and wipe up all anti-freeze spills. (Of course, if your dog runs loose all over the neighborhood, you have no control over what he might lap up, so keep him secure.) Almost 10,000 dogs a year die from antifreeze poisoning—don't let yours be one of them.

SUPPLIES

Now that your house and yard are puppy-proofed, and the whole family is ready to pitch in to help with the new arrival, you'll need to make a trip to the store to purchase some essentials for your Maltese.

As cute as they may be, it's not a good idea to give a dog as a gift.

Baby Gate

Impossible as it may be to believe, there are times when it's better to keep your Maltese in a separate room. That's where a pet gate comes in handy! They come in wood, wire, plastic mesh, and vinyl covered wire mesh, and can be either hardware mounted or pressure mounted. Some are expandable and some are one-touch. You have only to consult your own needs and taste to find the perfect one for your home.

Bedding

Hopefully, your Maltese will consider his crate the best place to go to when he needs rest or privacy. The addition of a washable soft pad should make the crate a cozy bed for your puppy. Look for crate pads that are made of soft, silky fabrics. Cottony and wooly fabrics can cause static electricity and contribute to hair breakage, something that show people really worry about.

If your Maltese won't be using his crate as his regular bed, you will want to purchase a special, comfortable dog bed for him. Many experts believe that it's important for a dog to have his own bed, designated for his use alone. Beds come in an almost unlimited variety of styles, colors, and fabrics. (If your dog is chewer, stay away from wicker.) Buy a bed that is as long as your dog is when he's stretched out. If your Malty likes to sleep curled up, a small bed with raised sides might be just the ticket. Dogs who prefer to stretch out at night generally like a rectangular bed without the high sides. There's even an allergen-resistant bed, made from "breathable" nylon, a washable fabric tougher than cotton or fleece that traps dust and other allergy causing particles

In the long run of course, whatever bed you choose may not matter that much, since your Maltese will spend as much time as possible sleeping on your lap. That's why you have a lap, isn't it?

Carrier

A pet-carrier is an absolute must for your Maltese. With a handy carrier, you can carry your Malty everywhere. (Some people consider them an alternative to leashes, but keep in mind your dog does need some exercise!)

You can even find backpack carriers for hiking and wheeled bags for air travel. For extra comfort (at least for the dog) there are front-pouch carriers, which can easily handle a Maltese. My own favorite is the Sherpa bag, which has soft sides and a strong shoulder strap—very chic indeed. Some carriers double as a car safety seat and are easily belted into any automobile. Many include storage compartments for food, water, and other pet supplies.

Choose a carrier that suits your needs. For air travel, if you have to check your Maltese like a piece of baggage, you will need a hard crate. However, if you can bring him into the cabin with you, a soft carrier will work very well.

Collar and Leash

To keep him safe and secure, your Maltese will need a leash and collar. Collars come in several materials, including leather, metal, and nylon. Leather and metal collars are not recommended for your Maltese, since these types of materials cause the long hair around the neck of the Maltese to break. Choke chains are also not recommended for your Maltese—they can be too heavy for your small dog's neck, and can damage the trachea.

A thin, flat nylon collar with a buckle will work best with the silky white mane of the Maltese. Nylon comes in many colors and prints, so you can have fun and make a great fashion statement, while keeping your Maltese safe.

When it comes to collars, fit is everything. The collar should be tight enough so it won't slide over the dog's ears, but loose enough so you can fit two fingers between the collar and the dog's neck. Make sure that you check the fit of the collar often, especially if you have a fast-growing puppy.

When you walk your Maltese, he needs to be on a lead. Even the most clingy, obedient dog can run off in a split second when he spies a chattering squirrel across the street—keep him safe and prevent accidents by using a leash. It's best to get several

Visit Your Vet!

Within 72 hours of purchasing your Maltese, make an appointment with your veterinarian for a complete checkup. You should have already researched and found a veterinarian for your Maltese (your breeder or local kennel club are great places to get recommendations.) Although a good Maltese breeder will have already given the puppy a health check, you need to schedule your own exam as additional security against health defects—problems that may not have been apparent the first time. If your vet offers microchip ID implants, this an excellent time to get one. You should also discuss with your veterinarian plans for spaying or neutering your puppy when he is older.

lengths: a short leash for congested areas, and a longer one for parks and country walking. As with your Maltese's collar, select a lead that is made from a lightweight material like nylon. Alternately, many Maltese owners prefer to use the loop type one-piece show lead that has a slip knot closure. These show leads can be purchased online, at dog shows, or through your dog trainer.

Harness

Instead of a leash attached to a collar, some Maltese owners prefer to walk their dog with a harness. Harnesses seem especially popular for puppies; they are also good for dogs with spinal problems, delicate necks, or for sensitive dogs who don't like collars. They are safe, but provide less control than other methods.

Crate

When dogs lived in the wild they slept in dens, which were often nothing but shallow holes in the ground. A crate is simply a modern version of the den, where a dog can feel comfortable and secure in a place of his own. Crates aren't a "puppy prison," and used judiciously, they can improve the speed of housetraining. Also, crate training makes traveling with your Maltese much safer.

Types of Crates

Your Malty's crate will be his home, hiding place, traveling compartment, refuge, and housetraining tool. Crates come in many varieties: heavy-duty wire, sturdy plastic, fiberglass, and even fold-up nylon varieties that are super for travel. Many dogs prefer the wire crates, which offer good visibility and ventilation. If you choose a wire crate, look for a sturdy one with heavy gauge wire that can be easily folded down into a "suitcase-style" shape for transportation and storage. Keep in mind that wire crates are not approved for airline travel.

Other dogs seem to prefer plastic crates with their close, den-like atmosphere. The weather is a factor too—wire crates are better ventilated, but if it's a wet day a solid-plastic crate is best. They are also less expensive than wire crates, and most plastic crates meet federal regulations for airline travel.

Safety Tip

Make sure that you clean under beds, and clear off tables or other areas where there may be small items that can be ingested by your tiny Maltese.

Most modern crates, both plastic and wire, can be easily taken apart or folded up for storage. All crates should be well ventilated and provided with comfortable, easy-to-clean bedding. For extra comfort, put an old, unwashed tee shirt or bathrobe that holds your scent in your Maltese puppy's crate.

Whether or not your puppy should sleep in his crate is a matter of dispute and individual preference. Certainly your dog should learn to accept being crated; otherwise travel, surgical recovery, and other eventualities may be unduly trying. Your puppy is safe in his crate (and so is your house), but there's nothing wrong with having your puppy sleep in a bed with a family member (as long as it's agreeable to the family member).

When it comes to size, you want to make sure that the crate is big enough for your Maltese to stand up, turn around, and lie down comfortably. However, one that is too large can be a disadvantage if you're using the crate as a housetraining tool. You don't want to give the dog room to "go" in one part of the crate and sleep in the other.

Clothes

While some people prefer that their dogs go naked, the Maltese wears clothes remarkably well. Dog clothing comes in two basic sorts: the utilitarian and the decorative. Some items, of course, do double duty. A beautiful coat can help keep your little dog warm in the cold winter months, and cute boots are more than just fashionable—they protect your Malty's feet from snow and ice.

Since the Maltese is a white dog, almost any color suits him, although I have a preference for blazing red and classic black. I would even consider a pattern—with a Maltese Cross motif, of course.

If you are handy with a needle and thread, your choices are

Make sure your Maltese has a comfy place of his own to sleep.

You may decide to purchase a dog bed fit for a princess!

unlimited, but for those of us who are less than adept, we can still join in the fun. Every pet supply store in the world has a dog-costume section, and the internet is well supplied also. There's no need to wait for Halloween, either. The year is replete with opportunities to dress up your dog! Superbowl, Groundhog's Day, Valentine's Day, March Madness (for basketball fans), Easter, May Day, Flag Day, Independence Day, Christmas, his birthday (or "Gotcha Day" for adoptees)—the sky's the limit.

In addition, there are rain and snow outfits, sun hats, sweaters, and bikinis available for your Maltese. Go ahead, have fun—as long as your Maltese enjoys his canine couture (and many little dogs do). As to those who think costumes are beneath a dog's dignity, well, they're just missing out on the fun.

One word of warning: Don't let the kids dress up the dog without your consent and supervision, and never leaver the dog unattended while in an awkward or draggy costume.

Ex-Pen

The exercise pen or "ex-pen" is an excellent way to give your dog both freedom and security. This portable wire play pen is an excellent addition to your dog supplies, especially if you travel with your Maltese. You can confine him safely while you enjoy a sandwich at the rest stop.

Grooming Supplies

Good grooming is essential to your Maltese's health and looks, and so it's wise to invest in the very best tools you can afford. At the very least you will need:

- A grooming table if you can afford one. It will save your back and restrain your Maltese.
- A good pin brush with pins long enough to penetrate the Maltese's coat.
- Mat detangler.
- Several steel (not plastic) combs, including a flea comb. Steel

works through the Maltese hair much more easily than plastic. You may want to get several sizes.

- A triangular shaped slicker brush. The triangle shape helps get into those tricky little places, like the "armpit."
- Scissors (6 inch/15 cm). Your can use the ones made for people-hair. If you want to get fancy you can add a smaller curved-blade pair.
- Water-repellent grooming smock to keep hair and water off you.
- Nail clippers and file.
- Styptic powder.
- Small rubber bands to hold the face hair.
- Grooming/conditioning spray.
- Tearless shampoo (you can use stuff made for a person) for the face.
- White dog shampoo with bluing.
- Conditioner.
- Product to help remove tear stains.
- Blow dryer and towels.
- Dog toothpaste and brush.
- Cotton balls for ear cleaning.
- Ear powder and cleaner.
- Tweezers.

It's also a good idea to invest in a good quality vacuum cleaner and plenty of lint rollers or other hair picker-uppers.

Toys and Chew Toys

Fifty-nine percent of dog owners buy toys for their dogs, according to the American Pet Products Manufacturers Association, and surely you will be one of them. It's a good idea to provide your Maltese with a variety of toys—they can help deter him from playing with items you don't want him chewing (like your socks, dress shoes, morning paper, or DVD collection), and toys can also help relieve boredom when you don't have time to play.

Chew toys are essential, especially when your Maltese is teething—a time when your little guy seems to have an insatiable chewing appetite. Make sure you choose a chew that is the appropriate size for your little dog. For a Maltese up to the age of six months (when teething is the most painful), you might want to purchase a chew toy that you can freeze for relief from teething pain.

Chewing Tip

Puppies love to chew! Make sure your Maltese has plenty of appropriate chew toys or you might find your antique Chippendale chair a goner. Some people use bitter apple spray, which can be purchased from any pet supply store, on furniture legs, woodwork, and other immovable items to discourage chewing.

Prevent a Lost Dog

Any time you bring your Maltese outside, he should wear a flat nylon collar with a buckle, plus his identification and registration tags.

In addition to chews, purchase some toys that you and your dog can play with together, such as balls and plush toys. Look for toys that squeak and are interactive to keep your Maltese stimulated, but always be mindful of the size. I've found that Maltese particularly like to bat and chase fuzzy plush soft toys. However, if your Maltese prefers to tear and chew rather than push and carry, choose a tough rope toy, which is also good for the teeth. You might also consider a leather toy, which usually does no harm if swallowed.

It's always a good idea to supervise your dog when he's playing with any toy. Avoid giving your Maltese a toy that has small, detachable parts, such as a doll with eyes that can be chewed off. Even though your Maltese is small, those sharp teeth have more chewing power than you might imagine. If your dog ingests small parts from a toy he may end up with a serious internal blockage, which could require surgery. When your dog does tear up a toy, be sure to throw it away.

Water and Food Dishes

You will need small lightweight bowls for food and water. Bowls can be made from metal, plastic, or ceramic. Some Maltese fanciers avoid using plastic bowls, believing they may cause facial hair stains. Most people choose stainless steel bowls, which

Owners of purebred show dogs have long used tattoos to provide permanent, visible identification should their dogs get lost.

are attractive, less expensive than ceramic, and easy to clean. Ceramic bowls come in many fashionable and fun patterns, but they tend to be more expensive and can break if dropped.

Because of the hair around the Maltese's face, when this breed drinks from water dishes the facial hair can get wet and sloppy. The wet facial hair can be a breeding ground for yeast, which causes tear staining. Some Maltese owners prefer to train their dogs to drink from a water bottle (like those used for rabbits or guinea pigs) to avoid this problem.

IDENTIFYING YOUR MALTESE

ID Tags

Your Maltese is worth a lot, even if you got him for free. To protect your new friend, you should make sure he carries ID at all times. No matter what additional kinds of identification you may use, outfit your dog with a flat collar and tag that carries your name, address, and phone number. You can also put the information right on some kinds of collars with a simple laundry marker, so you dog will be identified, even if the tags are ripped off somehow.

Tattooing

Owners of purebred show dogs have long used tattoos to provide permanent, visible identification should their dogs get lost. In this form of identification, a tattoo is etched on the inside of your Maltese's thigh near his abdomen.

Microchipping

The latest technology allows you to microchip your Maltese. The microchip cannot get lost, nor can it be altered. The microchip is only the size of a grain of rice, encapsulated in a special bio-compatible material that allows your dog to wear it safely under his skin. Your veterinarian injects it between the shoulder blades; the dog does not have to undergo anesthesia for the process—it's quick and painless. Once it's implanted it's there— no batteries required. The number of the microchip is entered into a database, so your Maltese can be identified. (You'll need to notify the company if you move or if the dog's ownership has changed.)

If your dog gets lost, veterinarians or humane society personnel have handheld scanners that can be passed over the dog. If a microchip is present, its number will be displayed on the scanner. Of course, not everyone who finds a lost dog has a scanner or knows enough to take the animal to a vet or humane society that does. Therefore the microchip does not replace traditional ID tags!

TRAVELING WITH YOUR MALTESE

One advantage to having a Maltese is his portable size—he can go practically anywhere with you, as long as you plan ahead and take some precautions.

Staying in a Hotel or Motel

Believe it or not, not every hotel or motel in the world will welcome your Maltese (I guess they haven't yet gotten the word that this is the best breed on earth). Before your trip, call ahead to verify that the hotel or motel currently accepts pets. Just because they did *last* year doesn't mean they do this year.

Even hotels that welcome pets may have limits on the number

Using a crate is the safest way to travel with your Maltese.

of dogs permitted. Some require that the dog remain crated if left alone in the room. Some require an extra deposit or charge additional cleaning fees. When you call ahead, be sure to ask about the hotel's policy, and be honest with the hotel about your four-legged friend. When making your room reservations, get confirmation in writing that having a dog in the room is allowable. You don't want to show up and be told that there must be some mistake and dogs aren't allowed.

Make sure you and your Malty never leave the hotel room unless he is on a leash or in your arms. Many of the hotel's other guests may be afraid of dogs (yes, even Maltese), and the leash is reassuring to them. And of course, clean up after your dog after every outing. Don't allow your dog to bark or scratch at the door. If you have to, keep him safely in a crate.

Keep your dog clean and well-brushed. The more you brush him outside, the less he'll shed inside, and that's good news to the cleaning people. Remember, you don't want dogs to get a bad name. Make his stay hassle-free for everyone. And when you leave, give a nice a tip to the cleaning folks. Leave them with a positive feeling about your Maltese.

By Car

Most Maltese enjoy car travel, but if he's unaccustomed to it, take him for some practice runs before the big day. Feed your Maltese about one third what you normally would before starting out, to reduce the chances of his getting sick. (But bring some extra food or snacks with you on the trip.)

Safety First

Of course, safety is paramount. You don't want your Maltese to turn into a fluffy football flying through the windshield if you have to brake for a deer. Just because your dog is small, doesn't mean he can't cause one big accident. Even if your dog rides quietly, remember that, in a 30-mile-per-hour collision, a dog can exert a force 20 times his body weight. And even if your dog doesn't go flying through the air, a loose dog in a car is a driver distraction.

The best way to travel with your Maltese is to put him in a crate in the back seat. Secure the crate by running a seat belt (without a shoulder harness) through the handle of the crate,

> **Crate Tip**
>
> No puppy should be in a crate longer than a couple of hours except at night. It's too confining for a lively young dog and will stunt his mental and physical growth. Dogs need stimulation!

then fastening the belt. Some people use seat belts, but they aren't always very effective for small dogs. If you do use a safety belt, choose one with a metal rather than a plastic buckle that can break on impact. Another problem with safety belts is that a very active dog can get twisted up in them. Another choice is a canine car seat designed for small dogs, such as the Buddy Booster, which allows your little dog to look out the window safely.

Some people simply put the dog in the back of the vehicle with a gate that prevents his getting into the passenger section. While this allows the dog freedom of movement without annoying you, it won't protect him into case of a sudden stop, and also exposes him to the risk of being thrown from the car.

On the Road

Whenever you take your Maltese out for a trip, think, "Hmm, what if my car breaks down on the road?" Be prepared for that happenstance. Your travel plans should always include:

- An extra leash.
- A supply of drinking water and a bowl.
- Any medication needed for the dog.

Even if you don't break down, be prepared to stop—about twice as often as you'd need to for a little child, or about once every two hours.

Of course you must never leave your Maltese in a hot car, not even for a few minutes. Temperatures can hit 120°F (49°C) in a closed car even with the window partly open. Temperatures below freezing are dangerous for Maltese too.

Under no circumstances permit your Maltese to ride with his mug hanging outside car windows (even if he can reach them), charming as the sight would be to fellow drivers. Not only would he be a distraction for other drivers, debris or other trashy particles can get into your dog's eyes to injure or infect them.

Car Sickness

While most Maltese love to ride in the car, some experience car sickness. In a few cases carsickness has a physical basis, usually caused by a problem in the inner ear. In that case, you can safely use an over-the-counter motion sickness medication like Dramamine (ask your veterinarian for a safe

Your Maltese may end up being a huge sports fan!

dosage for your Maltese). More often, however, the cause of car sickness is psychological. Perhaps the dog associates riding in the car with unpleasantness (like going to the vet). Or perhaps he is frightened of the noise or motion of the car. Sometimes it's hard to figure

Traveling with your Maltese is a breeze—just don't let him drive!

exactly what came first—the sickness or the fear. Dogs who are anxious may express their anxiety through sickness, and those that get sick in the car may become increasingly anxious about it. Usually (not always) if the dog shows signs of anxiety (slavering, shaking) before even getting into the car, the problem is most likely based in anxiety.

To help your dog overcome car fear, take it slow, and make the car a happy place. Try feeding the dog treats inside the car while the car is not running. Do this often enough for the dog to regard the car with approval. If your dog is even afraid to approach the car, you'll just have to give treats closer and closer to the car until the dog finally overcomes his fear. This may take some time.

Then repeat this routine with the car running. Go slow— trying to hurry the desensitization will backfire (hopefully not literally) on you. When you actually start moving go for *very* short trips where you get out of the car and take your Maltese for a walk. Do this every day until the dog starts to really look forward to his daily car rides.

If your dog still retains a fear of the car, you may have to resort to a medical solution. As mentioned above, I have always had great luck with Dramamine. You can also try non-prescription products like Pet Calm, Rescue Remedy, or Serene-um. (Always read the directions on the label dose according to the weight of your dog.) You can also try simple ginger in the form of capsules, bulk dried ginger, or ginger extracts, all available at health food stores. You can mix the dried or powdered herb into his food. Even ginger snap cookies might help! Calming herbs like chamomile can also be effective. In a few cases, you may need to get out the big guns and ask the vet for an anti-anxiety medication.

By Air

Your Maltese is a perfectly portable pet. His small size means that if you ever need to travel by air, more than likely he'll be able to travel with you in the cabin. Many airlines allow a dog to accompany the owner in a crate or carrier that is small enough to be stowed under the seat. However, rules vary. The safest thing to do is to call the airline and check *before* you fly as what that particular airline's requirements will and will not allow.

Before you even book your flight, check out the airline's policy about pets—you may need to supply a health certificate and a valid rabies certificate, which you can get from your veterinarian.

If for some reason your Maltese can't fly in the cabin with you, you can help reduce the risk of potential damage by following the law and using common sense.

- Try to book a nonstop, midweek flight.
- Try to fly during the evening or morning when it will be coolest.
- It's probably not a good idea to tranquilize your dog before the flight—it interferes with the breathing mechanism (the last thing you want) and even under the best of circumstances, it may take a few days for your dog to recover. Instead, distract your dog with cheese or peanut butter-filled treats that he will need to work to get out.
- Keep your dog's nails short for the trip—you don't want them getting snagged in the carrier door.
- Make sure your dog is flown as "baggage" (bad as that sounds) rather than as "freight" (which is worse). If he goes as freight he may be shipped on a different plane.

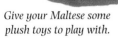

Give your Maltese some plush toys to play with.

Most airlines are also quite picky about the crate in which your Maltese will be flying. General rules are that the crate must:

- Be big enough to allow the dog to stand (without touching the top of the cage), turn around, and lie down.
- Have handles.
- Have a leak proof flooring covered with absorbent material.
- Be clearly labeled with your name, home address, home phone number, and destination contact information, as well as a designation of "Live Animals," with letters at least one inch high and arrows indicating the crate's upright position.
- Be ventilated on opposite sides, with exterior rims and knobs so that airflow is not impeded.

Get the crate well in advance so your dog can get used to it before the big trip.

Airline flight regulations in regard to pets change all the time. Contact the air carrier in advance for specific instructions. For more specific information about particular airlines, go to: www.akc.org/news/airline_chart_0504.pdf.

WHEN YOU CAN'T TAKE YOUR MALTESE WITH YOU

It is not always possible or even desirable to bring your Maltese along on every trip you take. In that case, you'll need to have a plan. If you're lucky, you can pop him over to mom's, but that's not an option for everyone.

Boarding Kennel

When you travel for extended periods of time, a boarding kennel may be your best option. Just as with other dog care options, it is important that you research them fully and are referred to them from reliable sources.

If you decide to use a commercial kennel, ask for a tour before you commit yourself—but commit early. Most kennels fill up a month in advance. Before you leave, you should also find out when you will be able to pick up your dog—many do not have Sunday pickup.

Lost Dog

While no one ever intends to lose a dog, it can happen. To help retrieve your Maltese as quickly as possible, keep a recent photo of your dog on file, either as a print or digital image. It's also smart to prepare a few dozen flyers before the dog actually gets lost, so you are immediately prepared to paper them around the neighborhood and at the local veterinarians' offices. Take one to the shelter too. Don't simply call them and ask if your dog is there. While they'll try to be helpful, some shelter workers won't know a Maltese from a Manchester Terrier. Take them a flyer and look at the found dogs for yourself.

If you lose your Malty, don't wait around. Take immediate action. The longer your dog is gone, the less chance you have of getting him back. Comb the streets, and enlist the help of neighborhood friends and kids. Maltese are not typically strayers or wanderers, so if he goes missing, it's possible that he has been stolen or injured. This is why checking vet clinics is critical. I can't stress enough that your dog should be wearing his collar and tag. Attaching a rabies tag is the law, so there's no reason not to attach his ID to the collar at the same time.

Good kennels:

- Are clean and free of excrement;
- Have both indoor and out door runs (preferably with solid partitions between each run);
- Allow dogs frequent access to exercise and play;
- Provide appropriate grooming and bathing services;
- Require proof of vaccination (or antibody titres), including bordetella;
- Have a vet clinic nearby for emergencies;
- Allow you to bring your dog own food, bedding, and toys if you desire;
- Are heated and air-conditioned;
- Are accredited with the American Boarding Kennels Association;
- Love Maltese and appreciate their unique qualities, and also understand their special needs;

Pet Sitter

Another option is a dog-sitting service. Some services house-sit as well as pet-sit; others make arrangements to come in and walk, feed, and play with your dog. If you are thinking of hiring a pet sitter, make sure to meet her first and note how she interacts with your Maltese.

You should do the following when interviewing a pet-sitter:

- Ask for at least three references;
- Ask her about her experience and make sure she will be able to walk, brush, or if necessary, medicate your dog;
- You may also want to test her knowledge by asking her how she might handle certain dog problems like vomiting or diarrhea;

If you like her, make specific arrangements about when she will be coming to care for your dog, and what else she might be able to do (like bring in the mail). Be sure she gets your contact information and that of your veterinarian. Let your vet know you are leaving and make arrangements for payment in case of emergency.

Dog Daycare

One of the great new options available to pet owners is doggy day care. If you work all day and your dog is home alone, you might consider driving him to doggy day care. Whether this would be once or twice a week, or every day, depends on his needs and your pocketbook. Most dogs love the idea of spending their days playing with other dogs, getting attention, and having their every need catered to. This is also a dream-come-true for busy working owners who *know* their dogs need more attention than they are currently getting. Instead of coming home to a desperate-to-go-out, anxious, and lonely pet, you'll pick up your happy, tired, and ready to be cuddled love-muffin.

To find a good doggy day care, check around. Your friends, veterinarian, dog trainer, boarding kennel, groomer, or kennel club may have some suggestions. Of course you should check out the facility before committing your dog to its care. Good day care has a low staff-to-dog ratio, is sparkly clean, and has plenty for your dog to do. The best places have safe indoor and outdoor play areas, nap spaces, and toys. While you can't expect a doggy daycare center to be totally silent (you wouldn't want it to be) it should not be filled with the sounds of whining, moaning, and shrieking either. Watch the staff interact with the dogs, and note the dogs' demeanor. They should seem happy to arrive and not appear frightened or lonely.

Ask questions about how introductions and socialization are handled, what health checks are required, and what is done about aggressive dogs. Some day care centers offer grooming and bathing services as well. Although doggy day care isn't cheap, it's within the price range of many people, especially if the service is used only once or twice a week.

If you must leave your Malty behind, make sure he's well taken care of.

4

FEEDING
Your Maltese

Probably more ink has flowed over the issue of nutrition than any other single canine topic. Debates include commercial dog foods versus homemade; raw versus cooked; "people food" versus dog-only food; bones versus no bones; chicken wings versus no chicken wings; supplements versus no supplements—these topics have all have stirred dog fanciers to varying degrees of frenzy. The good news is: *relax*. Dogs (even Maltese!) are scavengers by nature and can survive and thrive on a remarkable variety of foods. A good commercial dog food will probably satisfy his nutritional needs and keep him relatively healthy. It's when the debate swings to foods that may prevent cancer, enhance the immune system, and improve overall health that differing opinions make for good discussion.

You might think with his small size and delicate looks, the Maltese would have certain special breed-requirements for his food. Well, you'd be wrong—he has the same nutritional needs as any other dog, and eats the same amount as another small-breed dog who gets similar exercise. Small-breed dogs do have smaller mouths and will benefit from smaller sized kibble or meat chopped more finely than for a Saint Bernard, but that is about the extent of the difference.

WHAT SHOULD YOU FEED YOUR MALTESE?

When it comes down to it, what is the best kind of food for your Maltese? Check out any large pet store and you'll see a huge array of commercial food available.

Commercial food can be a convenient option.

Browse your local bookstore and you'll find many books on the health benefits of home-cooking or raw food diets. Let's take a closer look at some of your options.

Commercial Diets

Your choice of commercial dog foods is practically unlimited: dry food, canned food, semi-moist, or any mixture thereof. Many factors come into play when choosing which one might be right for your Maltese: convenience, expense, nutritional value, taste, availability, allergies, and other things. What's right for one dog is not right for all. One rule I do apply is, "Don't feed your Maltese something he dislikes." Yes, he will eat almost anything if he gets hungry enough, but so would you, rather than starve—that doesn't mean you'd like it. Mealtimes should be pleasurable for everyone, so why not shop around until you find something nutritious that your Maltese really enjoys? If he seems to like something for a while, then gets bored with it, change his food.

Dry Food (Kibble)

Kibble is a convenient, nutritionally adequate food for dogs. Dry food helps reduce tartar buildup on teeth, but keep in mind even on a diet of kibble you'll still need to brush your dog's teeth. This is extremely important for the Maltese, who like many other small breeds, tend to have crowded teeth and

Kibble as a Base Food

Some people like to feed their dogs a basic diet of kibble, and then add different foods every day, like green beans, carrots, or canned meat. This plan gives your dog adequate nutrition and also some variety.

get tartar buildup. Eating dry food doesn't help clean the canine teeth (the fangs), since chewing is done with the back teeth.

In comparison with other food choices, dry food is the least expensive, largely because of its high grain content. Dry food also tends to be low in fat. When choosing kibble, don't be seduced by fancy colors and shapes; your Maltese doesn't care about the shapes, and the colors usually come from dye, not food nutrients. What you do want to look for is a kibble small enough that your little dog won't have any trouble eating it.

Some dry foods are preserved with BHA or BHT. Although BHA and BHT have been established as safe by the federal government, many people question this finding. If you don't wish to feed your dog food containing these preservatives, you can find some dry foods that don't use them. Instead, look for a food preserved with tocopherols (vitamin E) or ascorbic acid (vitamin C)—the most common natural preservatives. These "natural" dry foods are usually more expensive, but they are becoming more widely available than in the past. Large pet store chains are even starting to carry these types of brands.

Canned Food

Canned food is much more expensive than kibble, and is usually about 75 percent water. The Association of American Feed Control Officials (AAFCO), which provides model regulations for pet foods, allows a maximum of 78 percent of water in canned foods, unless the food is labeled as "gravy," "sauce," or "stew." In that case, water content can be even higher! Canned foods may also be high in fat.

Canned food can be useful for mixing with dry food, since most dogs find them highly palatable. Dogs who have urinary tract infections often do better on canned dog foods than on kibble, mostly because of the increased water in canned foods.

Semi-moist Food

Semi-moist food is about 25 percent water, and can be just as high in sugar, in the form of corn syrup, beet pulp,

Don't Skimp on the Water!

Unless advised by your vet, don't restrict your dog's access to water, even if you think he doesn't really need as much as he is drinking. (One exception may be when housetraining your pup; you may limit his water access for an hour or so before bedtime.) If you have more than one Maltese, each one needs a separate water dish.

Food should be served at room temperature if possible, not directly from the refrigerator or a hot oven. Very cold food eaten rapidly can make a dog sick (not to mention that ice cream headache). On the other hand, some food seems more palatable to dogs if slightly warmed.

sucrose, and caramel. Your Maltese does not need this stuff—it promotes obesity and tooth decay. The shelf life of these products is also lower than either canned or dry food.

How to Read the Label on Commercial Foods

Although most dog owners feed their pets commercial foods, few of them know how to read the label. It may come as a surprise to learn that as far as federal regulations go, very little is actually required of pet food manufacturers. Companies are required to accurately identify the product, provide the net quantity, give their address, and correctly list ingredients. Pet food companies are not subject to quality control laws. You might find some security by looking for the AAFCO label.

AAFCO-labeled foods provide a guaranteed analysis of the food, calorie statements, and a nutritional adequacy statement. While this doesn't necessarily mean the product is good, it does mean that it's properly labeled. Critics claim that the testing that AAFCO performs is not particularly stringent, and is in no way tantamount to a controlled scientific study.

However, the good news is that the highly competitive dog food market is driving up the overall quality of commercial foods. Today, owners have more good choices than ever before; however, they also need to educate themselves to know what they're buying.

- **Meat Labels**: If an AAFCO labeled product has the word "Beef" for its simple name, it must be 95 percent beef, exclusive of water needed for processing. The same goes for chicken, fish, or lamb. These foods are all canned; no kibble is 95 percent meat.
- **"Dinner" Labels**: If the word "Dinner," or a similar word like "platter" or "entrée" is used, each featured ingredient must comprise between 25 and 94 percent of the total.
- **"With" Labels**: If the word "with" is used, the named ingredient must be at least 3 percent of the total.
- **Flavor Labels**: If the label reads "Beef Flavor," rather than "Beef," it need only contain enough beef to be taste-detectable (as if you were going to try it). The word "flavor" must appear in letters as large as those of the named ingredient.

General Guidelines for Commercial Foods

Although reading the label can help give some information for commercial foods, they can be difficult to decipher. Here are some simple guidelines when it comes to buying commercial dog foods.

- In general, don't feed dog food containing "by-products." Meat by-products are the part of the animal deemed not fit for human consumption, and while some by-products like beef trachea, are healthy, nutritious, and tasty to dogs, others aren't. Unless the label tells you what the specific by-products are, it's easier to avoid them altogether.
- Avoid food laden with grain or cereal by-products, especially corn or wheat, which while nutritious, can be hard to digest. These are technically called "fragments," but can appear in many guises on the label. Look for rice or brown rice as the second ingredient. As a rule, rice is more digestible to dogs than wheat or corn, and is less likely to cause allergies.
- Soy is a protein to which many dogs are allergic; stay away from it.
- Good food should not contain sweeteners, artificial flavors, colors, or preservatives. The best dog foods are preserved

Some people supplement their dog's commercial dog food with fresh vegetables or meat.

If your healthy puppy is getting good nutrition in his regular food, he should not need supplements, especially vitamin or mineral supplements. They are unnecessary and can even be harmful (unless, of course, your veterinariain prescribes them).

naturally with vitamin E (tocopherols) or vitamin C.

- Select food with the specific name of a meat (beef, chicken, turkey) as the first ingredient. Foods that just say "meat" or "poultry" should be avoided.
- Stay away from moisteners like propylene glycol, added to "chewy" foods.

Home-Cooked Diet

If you really want to go all out for your Maltese, you can't do better than a home-prepared diet of meat, eggs, and a variety of vegetables, with occasional additions of rice and yogurt, or perhaps fish. Vegetables like green beans, carrots, and potatoes are usually fine for dogs. A big advantage of homemade diets is that you can tailor it to your dog's particular needs. And you will be using higher quality ingredients than found in many commercial foods.

Although you might think that it is difficult to concoct a homemade diet that can match the years of research represented by commercial foods, this is really not true. After all, you've been cooking for your family all these years, without resorting to pre-packaged kid-kibble. (Haven't you?) If you are truly dedicated to cooking up your Maltese's dinners yourself, there are some excellent resources on the topic. You can check your local bookstore or the web for cookbooks and information on feeding a proper home-cooked diet.

Home cooking can be a lot of work, and may be more expensive than a commercial diet. As mentioned, nearly all dogs do very well on commercial foods, which can't be beat for convenience and cost. A good quality commercial food will be the choice of many pet owners for that reason alone.

Raw Foods

One of the newest trends in dog nutrition is the feeding of raw rather than cooked foods. Proponents claim that raw food is more natural and richer in vitamins, some of which are destroyed by cooking. People who feed raw food diets also say it is beneficial for dogs with allergies and inflammatory bowel disease. Like a home-cooked diet, you can find information on raw diets in cookbooks and on the web.

The drawbacks of raw food, in my opinion, far exceed any

benefits. In the first place, while it is true that raw food is a natural diet for a wolf, a Maltese is not a wolf. I suppose if you wanted your Malty to have a natural experience, he could run down a wild goat and tear it to pieces and then devour it. This may sound silly (and it is), but it simply underscores the fact that Maltese are civilized beings who enjoy their food cooked. Palatability tests have shown over

A growing number of people believe a home-cooked diet keeps their dog in the best of health.

and over that dogs prefer the taste of cooked food as much as we do. As for any vitamins that might be lost during cooking, dogs are able to manufacture all they need from cooked meat, just as we humans do.

One other drawback I see is that uncooked meat, fish, and poultry can contain disease-causing bacteria, such as E. coli, and parasites like Toxoplasma gondii.

Is Variety the Spice of Life?

Some nutritionists insist the canine system does better on one complete food, and that switching around could be upsetting to the digestive tract. They compare a dog to a finely-tuned car, saying that once you find the right brand of gas with the right octane, there's no point in changing. Some people maintain that switching dog foods makes a dog finicky.

Others, citing the fact that dogs are natural scavengers, believe that dogs enjoy variety, and even thrive on it. They argue that since we don't yet know everything about canine dietary requirements, it's actually safer to

change a dog's diet occasionally, to increase the chances that he's getting what he needs.

These proponents of the "variety is the spice of life" school think dogs are a lot closer to humans than they are to cars. I agree with them. Don't get trapped into feeding your dog only one food, even a good one. Here's why:

- **It's unnatural.** Dogs are hunters and scavengers by nature and are designed to feed upon a wide variety of foodstuffs.
- **It's boring.** Dogs don't like the same food day in day out any more than we would.
- **It may be unhealthy.** Studies have not been done long enough on a large enough number of dogs to guarantee that any single food is completely adequate by itself.
- **It may cause allergies.** Researchers believe that one of the best ways for your dog to avoid a food allergy is to consume a wide variety of foods from puppyhood on.
- **It may be impossible.** What if your dog becomes allergic to something in the food, or the company goes out of business, or they change the formula?

My own five dogs eat a little dry food, a little canned food, and a lot of people food, and they are all quite healthy. This could be coincidence, but in my opinion dogs like and need a variety of different foods, both for their emotional and their physical well-being.

Good to Know

Unfortunately, just because a product has "beef" as the first ingredient doesn't mean that the product is mostly beef. Most companies engage in a practice known as "splitting." If they can possibly do so, they will divide the cereal products into separate categories like "rice," "rice bran," and then "brown rice." Added together, there may be more rice than beef. But because the companies are allowed to list them separately, beef is listed first.

AGE-APPROPRIATE FEEDING

As your Maltese grows and ages, you should be sure you are feeding him the right diet for his age and activity level.

Feeding a Maltese Puppy

Select a small-breed puppy food for your Maltese puppy— that is, a food specifically formulated "for growth" for your little dog. You *can* feed your puppy a diet for "all life stages" but he'll need to eat a lot more of it to get the nutrition he needs, raising the risk of him becoming overweight.

Puppies between the ages of 5 and 6 months may undergo a growth spurt. The whole shape of their body changes, and they may *look* thin, even though they aren't. Don't worry about this, and don't overfeed your dog in a vain effort to get him to "catch up." Puppies of any age should not be fat; roly-poly

Puppies need protein to grow and build muscle.

can translate very fast into "unhealthy."

Puppies have particular nutrient requirements that differ from those of adult dogs. Small-breed puppies need higher levels of protein, fat, calcium, and phosphorus to support strong growth and good development of bones, muscles, and other tissues. Because the volume is limited by your hungry puppy's size, it's best to feed a highly concentrated food, one that will supply his energy needs without unnecessary bulk. Stick with a suitable puppy food that provides the correct amount of the following nutrients.

Protein

Puppies need protein to grow and build muscle. Most of the growth of the Maltese dog occurs in the first 6 months of life, much faster than a large-breed dog. On average, your little dog will gain 20 grams per day; by 10 months he has multiplied his birth weight by 20 times! His food has to supply all the energy needed for this fast development and high metabolism.

Puppies need a diet containing 25 to 29 percent average quality protein during weaning; after that, a food containing at least 18 percent average quality protein will support growth from weaning to adulthood. The higher the quality of protein, the less is needed to meet your dog's needs.

It used to be thought that excess protein would produce skeletal deformities. *This has been shown not to be the case.* In

Your Maltese may enjoy and even thrive on a variety of foods.

fact, foods containing even 31 percent protein are just fine, so long as the food contains the appropriate amount of calcium.

Fat

Commercial puppy food generally contains more fat than food formulated for adults. A growing puppy needs more calories than a similarly sized adult dog, and fat is the most efficient way to provide them. A tablespoon of fat has twice the calories as protein or carbohydrates. Food made of ten percent fat is usually sufficient for a growing puppy.

Calories

Puppies need a lot more calories, between 50 and 100 percent more per pound (some say between 2 and 4 times more per pound), than an adult dog, depending on the age and size of the puppy. At six months, the amount of food can be reduced to 50 percent more than for an adult dog. When your puppy has reached about 80 percent of his estimated full growth, you can reduce the food intake into just over what an adult of that breed would eat.

How Often to Feed Your Puppy

Puppies should be fed more frequently than adult dogs—three or four times a day, spaced as far apart as possible. The reason for this is although puppies need a lot of food relative to their body weight, their tummies are still very small, and they can't take much at one time.

At three months, you can begin feeding your puppy twice a day. Toy dogs, however, have a greater surface to volume ratio and use up more energy than bigger dogs. This is particularly true between the time of weaning and 4 months. It's not too much to feed these little guys four times a day.

Feeding a Maltese Adult

Eventually your Maltese puppy will grow into an adult, and you can stop feeding him puppy food. You can begin switching your Maltese to an adult food at the age of about 8 months to a year. Introduce new, adult foods to your puppy one at time, and do it gradually.

Stick to a Regular Schedule

Food should be offered at a regular time, and served in the same place every day, if possible. Dogs enjoy routine, and keeping to a regular feeding schedule reduces stress. It also prevents many housetraining problems. Most adult Maltese should be fed two small meals a day rather than one large one.

Some dogs do well on a free-feeding schedule, where the food is left out for your Maltese—available at all time. If your Maltese doesn't pig out, this may be satisfactory. However, it is trickier to monitor food intake this way, and impossible to do so if you have more than one dog. Generally, I advise against it.

Is Garlic Safe?

Garlic (allium sativum) is a plant containing over 100 chemicals. Garlic used to be a fad additive, and many owners still swear by it. Allicin, the substance responsible for garlic's characteristic smell, is considered to be the source of many of its pharmaceutical benefits. Garlic proponents tout its supposed effects as an appetite inducer, flea repellent, immune system booster, and possible role in treating arteriosclerosis. Most experts believe these claims are not warranted; however, a little garlic certainly won't hurt your dog. It does appear to be a flavor enhancer, but if you're feeding a dog a good diet, its flavor should not need to be enhanced. One note of caution: a whole lot of garlic can cause a serious but temporary hemoliytic anemia in dogs; however, it would require a half a teapoon (at least) in a meal.

Feeding a Senior Maltese

Senior Maltese require a higher level of protein than a young adult; choose a good commercial food designed for seniors. Some are low-fat for weight loss, as well. Talk to your veterinarian about a good senior food when your Malty reaches the grand old age of ten or so.

FOOD-RELATED ISSUES

While Maltese are no more food motivated than most other dogs, there are still some issues around food you'll want to watch out for.

Obesity

If your Maltese is too fat, look in the mirror—you only have yourself to blame. Your dog eats what you give him (unless he has learned to open the fridge himself and make a bologna sandwich). If the extra weight amounts to more than 15 percent over ideal body weight, the dog is clinically obese with serious attendant health risks. Obesity can cause or complicate other conditions like arthritis, respiratory disease, liver disease, diabetes, and heart disease. And in a kind of vicious cycle, an arthritic dog or one with the beginnings of heart disease is going to feel less enthusiastic about exercise, which is the best way for him to lose weight. If you are overfeeding your Maltese all the supplements in the world won't help your dog. The simple truth of the matter is that the fatter your dog is, the shorter his life could be.

Is Your Maltese Overweight?

How do you know if your Maltese is overweight? For a quick check on your dog's condition, look at him from above. He should have an "hourglass" figure. If your dog looks more like a rectangle from an aerial view, he's overweight. Rubbing your hands along his sides, you should be able to feel, but not see, each rib. You should also be able to feel the layer of subcutaneous fat beneath. Weigh your Maltese regularly as well.

What You Can Do

If your dog is too fat, he's not alone. Recent studies show that 80 percent of household pets are overweight. The American Animal Hospital Association rates obesity as the number one nutrition-related health problem in dogs.

The good news is that merely walking your Maltese every day can help him lose weight (and the exercise won't hurt you either!). Slow walking is not going to do the trick, though. It has to be brisk! Depending on your dog's condition, about 15 minutes is a good healthy walk. With an overweight dog, you'll want to increase the speed and length of exercise gradually. Another wonderful advantage of exercise is that it helps strengthen the bond between you and your Malty, and that's always nice.

You'll also want to cut out the snacks and lower his caloric fat intake, along with his exercise program. The first step is to cut out treats (or simply pop him a small raw carrot piece), no matter how much he begs. Make sure the entire family is on board with the program—no more table scraps and handouts.

All that hair can be deceiving! To check to see if your Maltese is overweight, look at him from above while he's standing.

It only takes one "cheater" in the family to ruin your efforts.

To reduce the inevitable begging, feed your dieting Maltese in several smaller meals a day. Or you can try giving half his allotment for breakfast, and then doling out the rest of it throughout the day. Be sure you measure the amount—this is not an instance when you'll want to guess.

Don't put your overweight dog on a crash diet, however. It's inhumane, dangerous and won't work. (It results in the infamous yo-yo effect.) The goal is to limit the weight loss to no more than 4 percent per week.

You can buy commercial dog food in "reduced calorie" varieties. Many diet foods have higher levels of fiber, so that your dog is eating the same volume of food as before, but with fewer calories. Follow feeding instructions on the label for "weight loss"—not maintenance. Before you start your dog on a weight-loss program, have him examined by a vet. Some medical conditions such as hypothyroidism or Cushing's syndrome can contribute to obesity.

Not for Maltese Consumption

Alcohol: Dogs will attempt to drink sweet drinks and the alcohol can kill them.

Bones: Raw and cooked bones can splinter and tear the intestinal tract. It's not worth the risk, no matter how much your dog likes them.

Chocolate, coffee, and tea: All these products contain similarly dangerous substances. Dark chocolate, which contains theobromine, is especially dangerous. Theobromine is also found in cocoa beans, cocoa bean hulls (landscape bedding), cola, and tea.

Grapes and raisins: These fruits contain a toxin that can damage the kidney.

Macadamia nuts: These contain a toxin that can produce temporary paralysis and muscle weakness in dogs.

Tobacco: Tobacco products can be fatal to dogs if ingested. Signs of poisoning develop within 15 to 45 minutes and include excitation, salivation, and vomiting.

Uncooked Dough: Bread dough can swell up inside your dog's stomach and rupture it.

Treats

If you are dealing with an overweight dog, treats should not be offered. However, if you have a healthy Maltese, offering him the occasional treat can help bond him to you. You should look for high-quality treats—they are usually more nutritious and usually have fewer calories than table scraps. I like to offer my dogs liver treats, since I feel they provide nutrients some diets don't supply. Biscuit treats are also good since they aid (a little) in removing plaque and tartar from your Maltese's teeth. The same can be said of some rawhide products, which have the additional advantage of satisfying your dog's urge to chew and relieve boredom. The best bones are cream-colored, not white. White bones are bleached, which adds nothing and may remove some of the

Look for high-quality nutritious treats for your Maltese.

natural flavor. Don't leave your dog unsupervised with rawhide bones, unless you know from experience that your Maltese eats them safely without tearing off large chunks, which can produce choking.

Other choices include edible bones that come in several flavors (like bacon cheeseburger). Choose the smallest size; it still may take your Maltese an hour or so to chew.

And of course you can opt for a rubber toy that hides treats to keep your Malty amused. Stuff the insides of the toy with your dog's favorite treat, like cheese or peanut butter. Your dog will happily spend hours trying to nose and lick out every last bit.

Feeding Multiple Dogs

If you are feeding more than one dog, make sure that each dog has his own special room or corner to eat in. Alpha dogs may bully submissive dogs away from a bowl, and two would-be alphas may fight over food. Even if you have two peaceable dogs who eat well together, it's better to feed them separately. That way, you'll notice if one or the other goes "off his food," often the first indication of illness.

Treat Tip

Use treats in moderation — they add to the total caloric intake of your dog. You can always resort to using bits of carrot or apple for treats as well.

GROOMING
Your Maltese

The spectacular long and silky coat of the adult Maltese does not come maintenance-free. To keep such a coat in show condition requires considerable dedication on your part. Count on spending at least half an hour a day with it. Even if you are a wash 'n wear type of dog-owner and decide to go for an easy-care clip for your Maltese, regular grooming should still be an essential part of life with your dog.

And, good grooming is about much more than good looks! It's about health too. Grooming is not just a quick brush and a rub down. It includes dental, eye, nail, and ear care. Every grooming session is actually a mini-health exam, and your best chance to notice lumps, bumps, infections, skin problems, breath odor, and other conditions that signal disease. In addition, a good grooming session is like an extended petting—your Maltese will thrive on it.

Before performing any grooming task, be sure you have at hand, in addition to whatever other supplies you'll need for that particular task: a water-repellent, lightweight grooming smock, a lined wastebasket, paper towels for spills of any kind, and a lint roller. The hair belongs on the dog or in the wastebasket, not on you or the floor or furniture. It's also a good idea to have a set of grooming clothes you use just for that purpose, although this might not always be practical.

BRUSHING

You should brush your Maltese every day, especially if he has a long coat. The longer you wait between brushings, the more difficult (and longer) each session will be. You'll need a pin brush and coat conditioning spray. Also, get out your apron or grooming smock. There's no need to be covered in long white hair if you don't absolutely have to be.

Use a pin brush and some coat conditioner to brush your Maltese.

How to Brush Your Maltese

To make sure you brush the whole coat, start with the underside, not the top, using a pin brush. This will make sure you get right down to the skin without irritating the skin itself. Brush with smooth long strokes and try not to "flip your wrists" at the end of the stroke, which can result in dreaded hair breakage. As you brush, continually mist the coat with a conditioning spray, which helps keep the coat from breaking. There's really quite an art to all this, best learned by watching someone groom a Maltese for the show ring.

Tying the Topknot

What is a Maltese without his signature topknots? In the US, Maltese adults are shown with two topknots. In Europe they are shown with a single topknot. Puppies also usually have the single topknot, since they don't have the amount of hair required to do the double knots.

Items you need to tie the topknot include:

- Rattail comb
- End papers or mesh cut in 2 inch (5 cm) squares
- Small pillow
- Rubber bands
- Hairspray or gel
- Bows

For the single (and easier) topknot, gather the hair just above the corner of each eye. Then use a rattail comb to part the hair about an inch above the eyes. Some people like to backcomb this hair for a little extra poof. Then secure with a rubber band and place a bow over the rubber band.

To make the double topknot, put the dog on a grooming table with his head elevated on a pillow so you can get a straight look (if you don't, you'll probably put the topknot too far back on his head). Using your faithful rattail comb, part the hair straight back above the outside edge of each eye. Make a part in the center and divide into two equal sections. Poof out each section with a comb and secure with a rubber band, then use hairspray to make it stick. Take a wrap and fold it in half. Put one side of the topknot into the paper, fold it over, and band it, but leave out just a few hairs from the inside. Take another wrap, folded in half, and put the second side of the topknot into the paper. When you do the second side, take the hairs left out from the first one and work them into the paper. That will help keep both sides together. Use gel or hairspray to finish, and, if you wish, attach a bow. The best way to learn how to tie a topknot is to watch someone with experience. Your Maltese breeder or groomer should be willing to show you how.

If all this sounds like too much trouble, that's what groomers are for.

The Matted Malt

The Maltese coat tends to mat, and there's no mistake about

Did You Know?

Maltese do shed, but since they are a single-coated breed, it's pretty minimal. You probably shed as much as the dog.

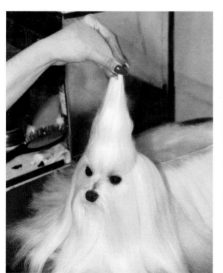

To make the single topknot, gather the hair and secure with a rubber band on the top of your Maltese's head.

To wrap the Maltese coat, comb out a section of hair, place the hair inside the wrap, start folding the wrap, then secure with a rubber band.

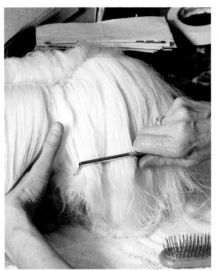 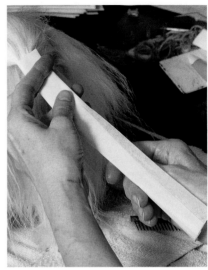

that. How much your own dog's hair will mat depends on the particular texture of his coat; it's a very individual thing. Some Maltese are "matters" and some aren't. If you find a mat in your dog's coat, try to work it out gently with your fingers first—don't attack it with a comb or mat breaker except as a last resort, since that inevitably results in loss of some hair. If the mat is too tough to handle with your fingers alone, spray it with a detangler or conditioning oil. Sometimes you have to let it soak in for a while. Once you've done all you can to that point, use the end tooth of the comb and work your way into the mat. If that doesn't work, use a mat-breaker, and promise yourself you'll be more attentive next time. Of course, if you don't care two cents about your dog's coat you can just cut the thing out (being careful not to cut the skin itself), but your dog will lose an element of his most striking characteristic.

Wrap Up

If you want to show your dog, you're going to have to wrap him up. Usually this process isn't begun until the dog is at least six months old (and most are older); before that the coat just isn't long enough to stay in wraps. A wrapped dog needs to be re-wrapped at least every other day or his coat will mat. It also critical to keep the coat dry while it's "under wraps" or, believe it or not, it can mildew and turn a hideous shade of green or even black.

 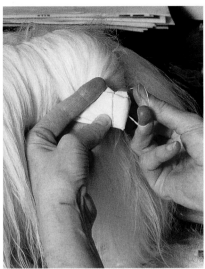 

Are you sure you and your Maltese are up for this? If so, here are your "wrapping supplies":

- Silk "wrapping" paper or bakery wrap paper
- Medium size rubber bands
- Rat tail comb
- Pin brush
- Conditioning spray

Put your Maltese on the grooming table and brush him out thoroughly with a pin brush. Take a well-parted, 2 to 3 inch (5 to 7 cm) section of hair (here's where the rattail comb comes in). Spray some oil or conditioning spray on it. Take the wrapping paper and fold about a quarter of it over to make an even fold, with the fold away from you. Put the hair on the wrap in the center, and then start folding the paper, first on one side and then on another over the hair. Keep the hair as straight as possible inside the paper. Crease the paper and then start folding the paper lengthwise. Soon your little Maltese will have a square of hair wrapped in paper next to his body. Secure it with a rubber band and then move on to the next section. You don't have to wrap the entire dog, although some people do. Others just wrap the hair that is most in danger of getting soiled or broken.

The Pet Clip

If wrapping sounds like way more than you want to do,

you can go in for a pet clip or trim for your Maltese. You can even do it yourself, although the majority of people choose a groomer. If you want to attempt it, I suggest you first have your Maltese clipped by a professional the way you like and then attempt to imitate the cut. One common practice is to use a clipper with a #4 or #5 blade and clip the whole body from the neck to tail. Use a downward motion to get a smooth finish. After this, use a #10 blade (the higher the number, the finer the cut) on the sides of the face. Clip from front to back. Clip under the ears, but leave the ears long, and trim the face so that your dog can have a charming moustache and beard. Trim the head so that he has a little cap. Trim the legs to blend in with the body.

Having said all this, I want to remind you that this is your dog, and you can have him trimmed any way that appeals to you. Go ahead, be creative!

BATHING

Stop! Did you brush your Maltese first? I hope so, because an unbrushed Maltese is almost inevitably a matted Maltese, and once you get a mat wet, it's all over but the cutting. Besides, with a good brushing you have eliminated a bunch of dead hair that you now won't have to bathe—very efficient, all the way around. Most Maltese should be bathed every seven to ten days, but of course a lot depends on how much he goes outside and how carefully you brush him in between baths.

Gather your supplies before you get your Maltese wet—you can't leave your Maltese in the sink unattended, and you don't want to be running around the house looking for a towel with a wet dog under your arm. You'll need: cotton balls, mineral oil, shampoo, conditioner, non-skid mat, towels, blow dryer, pin brush, slicker brush, comb, scissors, and a rattail comb.

How to Bathe Your Maltese

Luckily the Maltese is so small you can usually wash him right in the sink (no heavy lifting). Clean his ears first (see Ear Care, below) and pop a cotton ball into each ear to help keep them dry. You may also use a little sterile mineral oil in each eye to protect them and reduce the possibility of excessive tearing, which produces the dreaded tear stain. Put a non-skid mat on the bottom of the sink. Obviously you don't want your Maltese slipping and drowning.

Using the hand-held sprayer on your sink, soak the dog thoroughly and then apply the shampoo, preferably one designed for white dogs. I like Ultra White Shampoo, which is specifically designed for the Maltese coat. It not only cleans but also brightens and helps remove stains. However, in some cases, repeated use of a whitening shampoo over a period of time can damage and dry out the coat, so you may want to alternate with a more traditional canine shampoo. Don't be afraid to experiment with different kinds of shampoos and conditioners. Each dog responds differently.

Lather the dog down to the skin and wash from the back to the front. Don't forget the feet and private area. Rinse and repeat if necessary. Don't scrub in circles and damage the coat; modern products are quite capable of releasing dirt without a lot of "elbow grease" from you. Wash the face last, using a washcloth and tearless shampoo. *Rinse, rinse, rinse.* It should take twice as long to rinse the dog as to wash him. If you leave any shampoo in the coat, it will dull the dazzle.

You may decide to add a "coat-handler," which stays in the coat and helps keep it mat free, nice smelling, and free of

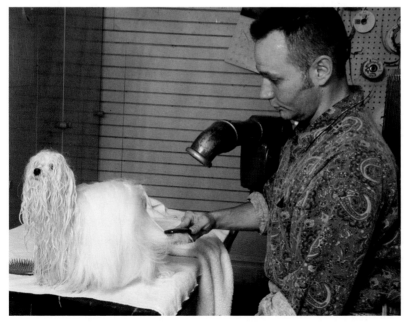

A free standing canine blow dryer allows you to brush your Maltese's coat while it's being dried.

static. If you use a traditional conditioner, let it stay in for the recommended length of time before you wash it out. In either case, use a light conditioner that is not going weigh the coat down.

Drying

After the bath, use your hands to remove extra water from the coat and then towel dry. Just hold the dog and press; don't try to rub him dry. Finish with a blow dryer. It might be nice to invest in a free standing canine blow dryer. The beauty of this is that it leaves your hands free to work on the coat. Set the temperature to warm, not hot, if you have a choice. High heat can result in coat breakage. Use the pin brush and brush the coat out in the direction the hair grows. Do only small sections at a time. Then follow by brushing the legs with a slicker brush. Do the face with a small metallic comb. Scissor trim the anal area about half an inch.

Now don't forget the "part." To get a straight part, you will have to get the dog to stand straight, not always easy to achieve. Stand behind the dog and use the tail of a rattail comb. Start at the base of the dog's neck and run it straight down the spine. You will end up with a very handsome Maltese!

Dealing With Ear Hair

The hair growing inside the ear can cause a great deal of trouble, and most Maltese experts believe that it should be removed in order to allow the air to circulate freely. However, some people claim that removing the hair actually makes the ear more vulnerable to infection; you may want to discuss options with your vet or groomer.

Owners who decide to have the hair plucked may go to a professional groomer, but you can do it at home as well, using a commercial ear powder. Take the ear powder and sprinkle a little into the ear canal, covering the hair. Wait few minutes to let the powder dry the hairs completely. Then pluck out the hairs with your fingers, tweezers, or a hemostat. Pull quickly! Oddly enough, this doesn't seem to hurt if you do only a few hairs at a time, although you think it would. Don't try yanking the hairs growing on the inside of the ear flap, however. That does hurt.

EAR CARE

The drop ears of the Maltese require special attention, as they are prone to infection and tend to have excess hair growing inside them, which is always a bit of a nuisance. Clean them at least once a week. One easy way to check your Malt's ear health is to smell those ears! Foul or yeasty smells signal an infection, as does redness, sensitivity to touch, irritation, or head-shaking or tilting.

How to Clean Your Maltese's Ears

Collect your materials, which should include cottons balls,

paper towels, or moistened gauze sponges. Use a commercial ear cleaner or a combination of vinegar and water (if you can handle the smell). Vinegar does a good job of killing many varieties of fungus, but it's not an especially good cleaner for bacteria. And Maltese ears seem especially prone to both kinds of infections.

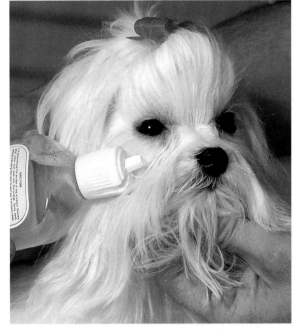

There are various products to help remove tear stains.

Avoid ear-cleaning products that contain alcohol, because they sting. Begin by cleaning the ear flap removing the dirt, wax, and debris. Don't use cotton swabs which can push the debris further into the ear. You're better off with thin wipes that mold to your fingers and work better to remove debris. Then, proceed to the cartilage. The doggy ear canal is shaped like an "L," so you will not be able to manually clean the entire ear; it's safest to just clean the parts you can see. If the ears are excessively dirty, you might buy a liquid commercial cleaner (again, one without alcohol) and use that.

Use a paper towel or dry cotton ball to dry the ears when you're finished; you do not want the dog to go running around shaking his head, as that can cause trauma to the inside of the ears. Repeat the procedure on the opposite ear. Then, give your Maltese a delicious treat to reward him for his "pawfect" behavior.

EYE CARE

While the eyes don't have to be groomed the way the ears and teeth do, you should still inspect them during the grooming process. If they are red, cloudy, or have a green or yellow discharge, you should contact your veterinarian immediately.

Do You Need a Grooming Table?

In a word, yes. Since you'll be spending a lot of time grooming your Maltese, it's best to do right, and purchase a proper table. You have dozens of choices, but a simple fold up one should serve your needs admirably. Use the smallest size on which your Maltese can stand comfortably; it reduces fidgeting.

Tear Staining

Many white dogs, including the Maltese, have unattractive tear staining. In fact, according to one study, 93 percent of 600 Maltese owners surveyed reported a tear-staining problem with their dog. There can be multiple causes (including genetics) but it often starts with a dog who produces excess "tears," which wet the fur around the eyes and create an environment perfect for various yeasts. Less frequently, bacteria in the tear ducts may be the culprits. In some cases the tear ducts can be clogged, a fairly common problem with toy breeds; they may have to be surgically opened. And, believe it or not, even an ear infection can "spill over," producing excessive tearing in the eyes—another reason to keep those ears in good order. In a few cases, allergies, especially to smoke, may case the excess tearing and resultant stains.

In some cases, the staining doesn't appear until the dog starts to cut his adult teeth. The eruption of the new teeth may be putting temporary pressure on the tear ducts. Usually the problem will clear up on its own as the dog matures, but it also helps to make sure your Maltese has a number of chew toys to help relieve the pressure. It helps to keep the face as dry as possible during this period, so the yeast responsible for the ugly brown-red color doesn't get a foothold.

Once you find the cause, there are a number of options available to get rid of the stains. The first step is to keep your dog clean with the hair out of his eyes. Make sure he gets plenty of fresh air and sunshine, too! If the air in your home is impure, consider adding a filter system. The whole family will benefit.

If the staining is caused by bacteria in the tears ducts, a ten day course of certain antibiotics may be helpful.

Face Staining

If you live in an area with a high mineral content in the water, you may find that simply drinking from the water bowl can leave a stain all over your Maltese's face and beard. Use bottled or distilled water and the problem will vanish. Some people even teach their Maltese to drink directly from a bottle, which has the additional advantage of keeping the face dry. Another way to avoid face staining is not to serve foods that are dyed or colored, because the color comes off on the face. Better quality foods usually do not have dye. Plastic bowls may also cause face staining in some cases.

Some that have been used successfully include tetracycline, chlortetracycline, delta AlbaPlex, neomycin, and Lincocin. In cases where the responsible agent is yeast, your vet may suggest otomax or xonodine. Some folks have also had success using collyrium, a mild, soothing eye wash that contains boric acid and buffers. It is available over-the-counter at most drug stores.

To remove the tear stains themselves, you can try any number of various commercial products now on the market. Select one that works best for you, or ask your vet or groomer for advice.

NAIL CARE

If you can hear your dog's nails clicking on the floor, you know it's that time again—time to get out the nail clippers and take care of your Maltese's feet. In fact, the nails should be even with the paw pad; anything hanging over should be clipped. Distasteful as it may be for your dog, it's important for his health that his nails are kept at a reasonable length. Untrimmed nails can cause the toe pads to splay and make it difficult for your dog to move properly.

You will usually need to clip the nails once every two or three weeks. The nails are softest just after a bath so that is a really good time to clip them. You will have a much easier time with this procedure if you start doing it regularly while your dog is still a puppy. But even if your Maltese is grown when you get him, you can learn to trim his nails yourself. If you've never done it before, though, ask your vet or groomer to show you how the first time.

It's also important that you have the right instruments for the job—in this case, a nail trimmer specifically designed for dogs. If you choose clippers, you can use either pliers-type or guillotine-type clippers, whichever you prefer. For small dogs like the Maltese, the guillotine type may be the most effective.

Nail Trimming Tip

Never use human nail clippers on a dog; they can splinter the nail.

In either case, make sure they are sharp! And please be sure to have good lighting—clipping nails is not something you want to do in the dark. You should also have some styptic powder on hand, in case you make a mistake!

How to Trim Your Maltese's Nails

If you're lucky, you'll have one of those super Maltese who will sit in your lap while you clip the nails. In that case you can actually turn the dog upside down while you clip; this makes it a lot easier. Others may need to be placed on the grooming table and restrained. If you don't have a grooming table, put the dog on top of the washing machine; it's slippery enough so that the dog is not anxious to fall off and he'll tend to stand very still.

The key to successful nail trimming is to understand the anatomy of the nail. Look carefully at the nail. Inside the center of each nail is the "quick," or the blood and nerve supply. You don't want to cut into that! Most Maltese have clear white nails, and the pinkish quick is very easy to see. However, some Maltese do have black nails, in which case you'll have to make several tiny cuts to reduce the chances of cutting into the quick.

Before you begin clipping, examine the toes for ingrown nails, soreness, redness, swelling, or discharges,

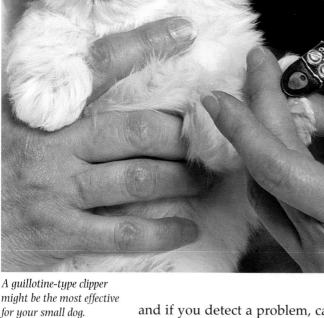

A guillotine-type clipper might be the most effective for your small dog.

and if you detect a problem, call the vet. If your dog's feet

have been overlooked for a while, the sensitive quick may have grown out very close to the tip. If this is the case with your dog, first try filing the nail every day for about three weeks. It's almost impossible for nails to bleed from filing. Filing will encourage the quick to recede enough for you to start clipping. You may want to continue filing every day between clips until you can get the nails as short as they need to be.

Electric Nail Grinders

Many people like to use an electric nail grinder. And oddly, dogs seem to prefer them as well, once they get used to the noise. Be careful not to use them for too long a period, however, as they can heat up.

When you are ready to trim the nail, cut the nail below the quick at a 45 degree angle. The cutting end of the nail clipper should be facing toward the end of the nail. If you make a mistake and clip the nail too short, use some styptic powder, flour, or cornstarch to staunch the bleeding. You can even stick the nail into a bit of bar soap! Hold with moderate pressure. After a minute or so, wipe away the excess powder and check the nail. If you don't take off the extra powder, it can harden into a kind of seal that will allow bleeding to start again when it breaks. If the bleeding continues for more than 15 minutes, call your vet.

One of the great things about nail care is that the more you trim your Malty's nails, the more the quick will withdraw back into the nail. This means there will be less of a chance that you'll cut into it the next time. Don't forget the dewclaws (the little fifth nails on your dog's front legs), if your Maltese still has them (in some cases they are removed while the dog is still a puppy.) If you like, finish off with a human nail file.

After you finish clipping the nails, take the time to trim out any scraggly hair growing between the toe pads. Otherwise that can mat up and even cause your dog to lose his footing. (This hair grows amazingly fast, by the way.)

DENTAL CARE

Brush your Maltese's teeth every day. I know it seems like a lot, but it's essential for your Maltese's dental health. Brushing every day helps prevent plaque and tartar buildup, which cause tooth loss, an extremely common problem in small dogs, who tend to have crowded teeth.

You'll need a specially-formulated canine toothpaste—don't use human toothpaste—and a canine toothbrush made for small dogs, or a finger brush.

How to Brush Your Maltese's Teeth

If your puppy or older dog is not used to having his teeth brushed, you may want to start by just putting some of the toothpaste on your finger tip, so the dog will see how good the stuff is. Let him lick it off—most dogs like the taste of canine toothpaste. Then proceed to sticking your finger into your Maltese's mouth to massage the gums and teeth. Once he's accepted this, it's only a small step to real brushing. You can use a

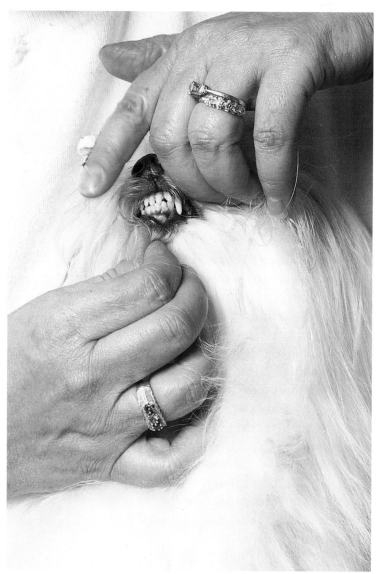

Dental care is essential to your dog's health.

canine toothbrush made for small dogs, but a lot of people find the finger brush easier to use. Put the toothpaste on the brush and start to go over the teeth, using a circular motion if you can. (It's a lot easier to just to brush back and forth, and it probably works as well.)

CHOOSING A PROFESSIONAL GROOMER

For many Maltese people a good groomer is almost as

important as selecting the right veterinarian. Although most professional pet groomers are able to groom a Maltese, some are much more competent than others. You can ask your veterinarian for recommendations, or check with breeders, boarding kennels, or friends with Maltese who are pleased with their groomers. Call the prospective groomer, and check on prices, products, and procedures. Also ask if the groomer requires proof of vaccinations.

Although a professional groomer can make your Maltese look exquisite, only you can do the regular ear, eye, foot, and tooth care that's necessary. Your groomer should be an enhancement to your dog's total care, not a replacement. Take time to watch the groomer with the dog. Any groomer who is rough should not have the care of your precious Maltese.

It is your responsibility to inform the groomer if your Maltese is fearful of being groomed, or if he doesn't like being left by you. If he has ever growled or snapped during the grooming process, the groomer needs to know this as well. Likewise, inform the groomer if the dog has arthritis, a heart problem, epilepsy, or any other condition that could be aggravated by the grooming procedure. Remember your groomer is a groomer, not a dog wrangler or trainer.

Professional Teeth Cleaning

No matter how thorough a job you do on your dog's teeth, it doesn't replace a professional cleaning once or twice a year (just as for people)! Tartar can collect well below the gumline, and it takes the vet's special tools to clean it all out.

TRAINING AND BEHAVIOR
of Your Maltese

Y ou, like many other Maltese owners, may be thinking "Do I really need to train my little dog?" The short answer is yes. Every Maltese should be a trained Maltese. This doesn't mean he needs to be ready to join the circus, but it does mean he should know and obey basic commands and act in a civilized way among company. Unfortunately, not all Maltese are trained Maltese. And that's too bad, because an untrained, unsocialized dog is a pest to his owner, an annoyance to guests, an object of scorn to passersby, and an embarrassment to the breed. Because of these things, an untrained Maltese is at greater risk of being given up or abandoned.

THE IMPORTANCE OF SOCIALIZATION

It is critical for your Maltese to get along with other dogs as well as with human beings. Dogs are basically social creatures, after all—they adapt well to a variety of living arrangements. Puppyhood, especially between the ages of 16 to 18 weeks of age, is the age of socialization. Take advantage of it by making sure your Maltese puppy has as many positive experiences with the world as possible. An isolated dog is a mistrustful dog. The more the exposure he gets, the more trainable, stable, and sociable he will be. This is a solemn obligation on your part. The Maltese is not as naturally sociable as a Beagle (although he's not a loner like a Chow Chow, either). He needs your encouragement to look at the world in an open positive way.

The best way to socialize your Malty is to take him out and about as much as possible. Different people, animals, and environments are your "socialization targets." Make sure any dogs he meets are fully vaccinated, because before your puppy is four months old, he's not fully protected.

Your dog should experience without fear the following kinds of folks: elderly or infirm people with canes, walkers, and wheelchairs, shouting people, timid people, joggers, bikers, people in uniforms and weird hats, babies, bearded people, and people of all races. He should also learn to handle different environments: other people's homes, parks, elevators, stairs, and high traffic areas (on a leash, of course). Make sure he's introduced to each new situation and person in a positive way, and don't overwhelm him. Taking your new puppy to you child's soccer game might seem like a great idea, but twenty rambunctious kids circling your Maltese trying to pet him may cause the opposite effect of your goal, and could make him fearful of children.

Puppy Kindergarten

One excellent start to socialization and training is to take your Maltese to a puppy kindergarten class, especially if you are a newbie to the world of dog ownership. Puppy kindergarten not only gives your puppy a chance to socialize with other puppies in a controlled atmosphere, but it gives you a chance to ask questions (maybe on housetraining) of a qualified trainer. Look for one who has graduated from training schools or internship programs, and who has some experience.

HOUSETRAINING

After socialization, housetraining is the most critical part of training a dog (some people even put it first). While not on a level with an aggressive dog, an unhousetrained dog can ruin your carpets, your friendships, and your life. And housetraining your Maltese quickly and correctly is in your hands.

Alas, housetraining your Maltese may be the hardest part of owning this breed. Many trainers put the Maltese on the top five of hard-to-housetrain dogs. As a rule small dogs are more difficult to housetrain than large ones, for several reasons. The first one is because they have tiny bladders that don't "hold it" as long as bigger dogs. So you must be extremely vigilant in taking your tiny Maltese out frequently enough. Second, because they are so tiny and don't eliminate much urine at a time, especially as puppies, it's easy to miss it if they do make a mistake. So you may think your puppy is housetrained when he isn't really. Here's the scary part: puppies under three months old may need to urinate every hour or two.

Setting a Schedule

To do this right, you'll need to get your puppy on a schedule.

Like babies, puppies need to pee a lot: after they eat or drink, after playtime, chewtime, or naptime. So, let's say Fluffy has just eaten—this is your cue to grab a leash and a tiny treat and head for the great outdoors.

Always use the same site for elimination. Your dog cannot only smell the scents from his previous trips, but also his memory of the spot will help trigger a natural function. Praise him quietly if he succeeds and reward him. Don't immediately head home, though. Many puppies need to "go" more than once during an outing. Besides, if he is enjoying himself, and you bring him right home, he'll soon figure out that the way to stay outside is to "hold it." Pretty soon, it will get to the point where he won't go for a really long time, and you'll decide that he doesn't have to go at all. You'll bring him in and he'll promptly poop on the floor. You can avoid all this by making sure that every walk includes some "fun." However, if a 15 minute outing produces no discernible results, bring him in for a few minutes, then try again.

Some people have had success by soaking up a little dog pee in a handkerchief and bringing it along on the walk. When they arrive at the spot where they want the dog to eliminate, they let the dog sniff the cloth and the dog responds in kind. I will leave it up to you as to whether you want to walk around with urine-soaked handkerchief or not. A better option are these little stakes you can buy in a pet supply store that have the scent of urine (undetectable to us, thank heaven) on them. Drive it into the ground where you want the puppy to go and you'll be amazed at the result.

Aside from his usual scheduled "potty break" times, you'll want to watch him carefully for any signs of wanting to go (like circling, sniffing the floor, or trying to hide), then take him out in a hurry and praise him when he succeeds. You can housetrain your puppy much quicker if you take preventive action like this.

Reliable housetraining may take several weeks, and some dogs just don't get it until they are nine months old. Pray for quick learner, but don't get discouraged—he'll get it evetually.

The Crate as a Housetraining Tool

Crate training is absolutely essential for this breed. Put the crate in a quiet area of the house, but one that is not isolated from the rest of the family. For housetraining purposes, the crate should be small enough so that he can't escape to the other side if he eliminates in it. However, I wouldn't keep a dog in a crate for more than a couple of hours, except at night, when he should be sleeping anyway.

Most dogs take to crates naturally, especially if that's where their bed is, but if yours seems hesitant, try feeding him special treats inside it. It's best to crate your puppy only for short periods and only (especially at first) when you are home with him. You don't want the dog to make an association between being in the crate and being left alone. Be sure your puppy completely eliminated shortly before your crate him—*and under no circumstances should your puppy stay in a crate for more than a couple of hours*. His sphincter is too weak to hold urine for much more than that, and he'll be driven crazy with boredom. If you have to leave for a long period, I think it's better to put the puppy in a puppy-proof room, like the bathroom, with plenty of toys to keep him occupied.

Never punish your Maltese for housetraining mistakes.

When You Can't Be There

If you are gone for long hours during the day, you should hire a dog walker to take your Maltese out for breaks. Otherwise your dog may either have an accident or suffer throughout the day. Consider how often you may need to use the bathroom yourself during that period. Do not deprive your dog of water, either, in the hope that will make an accident less likely. That is cruel and dangerous.

Another alternative is to gate off a tiled section of the house (like the bathroom or kitchen) and leave your Maltese there for the day. That will save you work, but will do nothing for his housetraining progress, unless you put your doggy litter box there (if you want to try that option). The same is true for crate training. While a crate is a wonderful housetraining tool, a puppy should not be left in one all day long. Puppies need mental and physical stimulation. The best plan is to put the puppy in the tiled area (which should be carefully puppy-proofed) when you are gone and also hire a dog walker.

Mistakes Happen

Do not strike or punish your Maltese for mistakes by "rubbing his nose in it." Just startle him by clapping your hands, scoop him up, and rush outside with him. Soon he'll get the idea. If you come upon the mess after the fact, just clean it up silently, and promise yourself to keep a better watch next time.

If your dog does make a mistake, it's important to remove all traces of the urine. If you don't, he'll be tempted to return to the same spot. If it's fresh urine, clean the rug with a good carpet shampoo. However, if the urine has penetrated through the rug to the pad beneath, it's unlikely you'll able to remove it completely. Good odor remover products like Nature's Miracle and Simple Solution, are manufactured especially for dealing with doggy accidents and contain enzymes to break down the odor-causing compounds in urine and feces. Follow the directions carefully, and let the cleaner soak in as deeply as the urine itself. You will have to keep the spot warm and wet for 24 hours. It helps to cover the area with plastic during this period.

If the urine has soaked into unsealed concrete, you will have to neutralize the urine (a product called Odor Mute may work) and

then seal the concrete—you may need professional help for this.

For hardwood floors, you should consult a professional, since enzyme cleaners may damage them.

Other Housetraining Methods

Some people use paper training or housetraining pads, and the Maltese is one of the few breeds for whom this might be a good solution, not only because they can be hard to housetrain, but because this breed doesn't do well in temperature extremes (and that includes rain). Simply put paper down where you want the dog to go and encourage him to use that spot by confining him to a room full of paper and then gradually reducing the papered area.

One of the latest rages is litter training for small dogs. It really does work and is very convenient if you live in an upper-level apartment or are gone for a large part of the day. Some actually function like an "indoor toilet" and come in two parts, a tray, and a grid. The grid allows the urine to drain away and collect at the bottom of the tray. Solid waste can be easily removed as well.

A potential problem with litter training is that it "breaks the taboo" of not peeing indoors. Some dogs may get very careless over time about this, and start eliminating everywhere! On the other hand, since it really isn't natural for dogs to eliminate inside, don't expect litter training a dog to be as easy as litter training a cat. The best way to address both concerns is to put the litter tray in a marginal area of the house, such as the utility or laundry room. Besides, who wants a litter tray in the kitchen?

POSITIVE TRAINING

Training your dog is an ongoing process. As your dog matures, learns new skills, and adapts to a changing environment, he is constantly being challenged. No dog is ever finished training, just as no human is ever finished learning. This doesn't mean training has to be an unpleasant or onerous chore. On the contrary, training your Maltese is the best way to bond with him, interest him, and expose him to an exciting world.

The best training for your Maltese involves positive reinforcement, usually in the form of food, petting, praise, or even play. Positive training is probably the world's oldest form of training since I don't suppose our ancestors went about striking or yelling at the local wolves in order to get them to obey. No, they bribed them instead. Punishment simply doesn't work very well for animals. If you want your dog to behave well, he will need to internalize good behavior. Punishment makes this difficult or impossible, because punishment is pain (either physical or psychological), and pain sets up barriers to internalization. For example, let's say a dog does something you don't like, such as snapping at a visitor. Yelling at or striking the dog creates an immediate unpleasant association in the dog's mind between the stimulus (the visitor) and the punishment. He will associate pain with visitors, and that will not make him like them any better. The old ways still work best—that's why they make dog biscuits.

Setting Rules

You and your family need to get together and decide as a group exactly what your dog will be permitted to do and what he won't. Maltese are extremely clever at figuring out the weakest link, and pushing his privileges first with that person. Soon the rest of the family gives up trying to lay any ground rules at all and the dog does what he wants. So you all need to decide—and act—together.

Make the following decisions before you even bring your Maltese home.

- Will the dog be allowed on the furniture?
- Will you let him sleep on the couch? Or on the bed?
- Will you let him beg for food?
- Will he be allowed to lick your face?
- Will he be allowed to jump up on your leg?
- What will be the rules for crating?

If you and your family can't decide what the rules are, your Maltese can't be expected to know either.

Consistency is the key to dog training. Once these rules are set, you must follow through with them. Your Maltese may not understand that it's okay to be on

You can use treats to positively train your Maltese.

the couch when the family is hanging out, but it's not okay when grandma is visiting; or that it's cute when he jumps up on little Sally when she's wearing her jeans, but not so cute when she's dressed in her junior prom gown.

Does My Maltese Need Formal Training?

As an addition (but never a replacement) to home schooling, is more formal obedience training. An obedience trainer will help you establish a communication system between you and your Maltese, help you teach your dog to understand and follow commands, and make sure everyone in the family knows who is boss (and it shouldn't be the Maltese). To that end, it's time to enroll your dog in obedience school— for his own sake as much as yours. Consider it this way: an untrained dog is an unpleasant dog to be around. He barks, paws, chews, begs, and bangs around the house. Your reaction will probably be to banish the dog to the yard, crate, or basement. What kind of life is that for a dog?
A well-trained, quiet, happy dog is a pleasure to be around, and you'll want him around a lot. In the end, you'll both be happier.

While many people do an effective job of training their dog at home, others do best with the structure and companionship of a formal obedience class. Don't select a trainer at random— get recommendations from trusted friends, veterinarians, or kennel clubs members. Check the trainer's credentials—many of the good ones are members of a professional organization such as the Association of Pet Dog Trainers. And visit a few classes without your dog. Participants (both human and canine) should seem relaxed, enthusiastic, and comfortable. Look for lots of smiling. Does the trainer seem interested in listening as well as talking? That's important. And since the training is for you as much as for your dog, work with someone with whom you have a rapport. The most effective trainers use positive reinforcement rather than punishment, so pay attention to how the dogs are being asked to do what is required. And of course the facility should be safe and clean.

Obedience classes help your dog learn the basic commands: sit, down, stay, come, and heel—commands not intended to turn your dog into a slave or robot, but become a functioning

Changing Food

Changing a puppy's food too quickly can produce some diarrhea, so if you need to make a food change, do it slowly, and be sure to take him out more often.

(and safe) member of society. You'll learn some things yourself, such as how to use your body, and tone and gesture to reinforce rather than contradict a command, how and when to reward or withhold rewards. Experience will teach you what rewards work best with your Maltese—some must have food, others are happy with a pat, or even a brief game. For some dogs the best reward is a chance to be allowed to run around and play with other dogs. Each dog is different, and as an owner you can discover a "hierarchy of rewards" for your own pet. Some classes also work on stopping problems behaviors, and some offer the basics in more formal obedience.

BASIC TRAINING

It's helpful to train your dog a little bit every day. It not only reinforces what he knows, but it also helps to relieve boredom and improves communication between the two of you. First decide exactly what the goal of the training session is going to be. If you don't know, the dog certainly won't. Make the goal attainable within a few minutes, which means that complicated commands may have to be broken up into "bits" over several days. A good rule for a puppy is that training sessions should last about ten minutes, and be undertaken three times a day. Any longer will bore or stress the puppy.

Doggie Door

If convenient, a doggie door might be the answer to your housetraining prayers.

Before you begin, have all the treats ready. Make sure they are good, soft, high-value ones, like pieces of cheese, not just bits of hard dog biscuit that take too long to chew. The treats go into a readily retrievable pouch or pocket. Pick a quiet indoor place (there are too many distractions outside) and a time when your dog is hungry but not starving.

The first rule is one trainer and one dog. It's impossible to train two dogs at the same time (the distraction is unbearable for everyone) and the dog will learn better if he has to pay attention to only one person a time.

Start the training with a brief review of something he already understands, and praise him for succeeding. Don't yell at your dog or wag your finger in his face. That will only upset or frighten him. Most successful training takes place in several steps.

- Get the dog to do the behavior (usually with a treat or some other lure).
- Speak the behavior (such as "Sit!") as your Maltese does it.
- Practice that behavior while using treats.
- Reduce the treat factor, changing the reward to praise.
- Make the exercise more challenging by increasing length, distance, or duration.
- Add distractions.

By now, your Maltese has morphed into Rin Tin Tin…at least sort of.

Always end the training with a success, even if you have to repeat something the dog already knows. Be assured that if the dog is not "getting it" either you are doing something completely wrong or you are trying to teach the dog to do something impossible, such as calculus.

It's important to end on a positive note. At your next training session, work on something different. Keep training interesting for your Maltese.

Basic Commands

Here are some basic commands you may want to teach your Maltese.

Watch Me

One of the first things your Maltese should learn is *Watch me!* Dogs are pretty good watchers, but training him to make and understand eye contact is immensely helpful. At first you may need to say, "Watch me" and move your head a bit. Remember that you are *a lot* higher up than he is. Reward the dog with a treat as he follows your motion. Soon he'll be watching you pretty much all the time and you can just reward with a treat occasionally.

You'll want to teach your Maltese some basic manners.

Come or Here

Come is the most useful of commands. It's purpose is to draw the dog to your side where you can watch him instead of charging off after visitors, visiting the cat's litter box, or hitchhiking to Buffalo. Start with the dog on an 18 or 20 foot (5.5 or 6 m) lead. Let him wander off, then call him to you while saying "Here, here, here!" in an excited, happy voice. If he comes, then give him a small treat or some affection; if he doesn't come, then gently pull him to you and reward him when he gets to you. Drill him over and over.

Litter-training Tip

Litter-training is not an excuse to avoid going outside with your dog. He needs to explore the wide world out there!

You can also try using a whistle to train your Malt to come. Start in a small area and bring your bag of treats. Sit right down in front of the pup and blow the whistle three times softly, then hand over a treat. This is basically the same method as clicker training, but Maltese can outrun the sound of a clicker pretty fast. Do this a few times, and then go play. Repeat a couple of hours later, standing further away from him this time. Soon he'll associate the sound of the whistle with you, petting, and treats.

Never use the *come* command to do something to your dog he won't like, such as bathing, fingernail clipping, or the like. Just go get him for those tasks.

Drop it!

This simple command is also a life-saver. Dogs are forever getting into garbage and poison, not to mention your own dinner. Start teaching him by waiting until he is chewing on an object that he really doesn't care that much about. (It should also be one that's not important to you, either, of course.) As he's chewing, go up to your dog, and say, "Drop it!" Offer him a treat in exchange. Practice several times a day, and always offer the dog a treat that he likes (like bacon)—better than whatever he is chewing. You want to reinforce that he'll be richly rewarded, not given a mere dry dog biscuit.

In real life, you would be most likely to use this command when the dog has gotten into something truly heady like a chicken carcass, so your established reward needs to be very powerful. Of course, you probably won't have any bacon actually on hand when the chicken carcass event occurs, but it's okay to cheat that one time and just reward him with a biscuit.

Success!

You can consider your puppy housetrained if he is over six months old and has not had an accident in a month.

Keep your puppy's training sessions brief and fun.

Afterwards, practice the *Drop it!* command several more times with your accustomed treat and plenty of praise.

Off!

It's a funny thing about Maltese. They tend always to be on what you want them off. The answer is not necessarily disallowing the privilege of furniture, but teaching them a positive rather than a negative command. Say, "Off!" in a cheerful voice, and offer him a treat on the floor. When he jumps off the couch, praise him. Of course, if you never want them on that piece of furniture, you can use your dark growly voice, but if you just want to move him temporarily, the *Off* command works very well. Or you can do things the easy way and just pick the dog up and put him on the floor. *Off* also works when you want your Maltese to jump out the car, as well. In fact, your dog should only leave the car when you command him to.

Wait

This calming command is useful when you have company. The dog doesn't have to sit, which can be very trying when friends have arrived, but merely to stand quietly and wait to be petted. It's also useful for keeping your dog from charging for the door while you open it—either to let someone in or to go out yourself. To teach the *Wait* command, begin by attaching a short leash to your Malt. This will serve to give you a little control. Touch your Malt quietly on the rump and say, "Wait" when a visitor arrives. Gently restrain him (if you have to), and reward him with a treat for quietly waiting to be petted by the guest.

Sit

Sit is an easy command to teach, but it is often used

inappropriately—usually when the owner really wants to dog to stay still, get out of the way, or not make a nuisance of himself. The catch-all "Sit, boy" is supposed to magically cure all the bad habits your dog has gotten himself into. It doesn't of course, and it's much better to work on actually curing your dog's bad habits (like jumping up) than to tell him to sit every time he does them. Think of it this way: Most of the time, when you ask your dog to sit, you really would be happy if he just stood there quietly. If that's what you want, that's what you must teach him. *Sit* is a useful command, of course. I ask my dogs to sit before I give them a treat, because it's easier for me to find their little mouths that way. It's also useful as a prelude to nail-clipping. And it's a simple trick for children to practice with the family dog, but it's no substitute for good all-around behavior.

The easiest way to teach *sit* is to say, "Sit" in a cheerful voice while holding a treat over your Maltese's head. Then gently start curving the treat backward over the dog's head. Most dogs will sit naturally. Praise him and give him the treat when his backside touches the ground. If he gets up too quickly, refrain from treating him. He needs to learn that the treat comes only when he is actually sitting. Otherwise, you'll turn him into a jack-in-the-box.

One of the first things your Maltese should learn is Watch me!

Down

This is the next logical command after *Sit*. If your Maltese is in the sitting position, at least you have the rear half down. The hard part is the front half. Most dogs dislike being asked to lie down, although they are happy enough to do it on their own. This is because *down* puts them in a physically and psychologically vulnerable position.

The Bow

Training your Maltese to "bow" is an impressive trick that's pretty easy to teach. Put a high-value food treat beneath your standing Maltese. As he starts to "bow" to get it, say, "Bow!" If he manages to get the treat without bowing, you will have to hold it in your fist, but in the same place. It's a bit awkward, but it works. Either way, praise the dog (or use a clicker, if you do clicker training) when he bows. Repeat several times, and pretty soon your dog will bow on command.

To teach *down*, put a treat in your hand, and while the dog is sitting, lower the treat slowly and move it towards the floor. Most dogs will lie down naturally. If your Maltese doesn't after a few tries, you can gently extend his front legs and praise him as you ease him to the floor. Don't push down on your Maltese's shoulders to force him down; you can actually dislocate his shoulder in trying to coerce a stubborn dog. Besides, you already know you're stronger than he is. You want him to perform joyfully, not out of fear or pain.

Heel (Walk Nicely on Leash)

Your leash is your dog's best friend. Don't think of the leash as a restraining device; think of it as a way to stay close to your dog. With only a little encouragement, your Maltese will look forward happily to the sight of the leash being taken off its hook: it means *walk-time*!

Begin your work with your Maltese when he is on a lead, not free. He should be responding to the *come* command before you start teaching him to heel, (which means to walk nicely on a lead at your heel.) Enforce your command if necessary by kneeling and using a treat to lure him. Don't pull on the leash. Only use the leash to keep him from going in the other direction.

It's customary to have the dog walk on your left side, so if you plan to engage in formal obedience training, you might as well start getting into the correct practice right away. Start by keeping a little treat in your left hand. The point is to get your Malty to believe that staying close to that appendage is likely to yield rewards. Since a Maltese is pretty low to the ground, however, bend down when you feed him. You don't want to get him in the habit of jumping up for the treat.

Treat your dog frequently as you walk along, but only when he's in the correct *heel* position. To help position your dog, hold the leash behind your thigh. Start walking in a counterclockwise circle. Since your dog will be on the inside, you'll find it easier to guide him as you move along. Say, "Champ, heel!" in a bright voice and start walking. Don't scold him if he goes in the wrong direction—just don't respond to it. Stay still or move in a different way. Soon he'll realize that all the rewards come from staying near you.

After your Maltese becomes accustomed to walking on the leash, and you don't have to give him a treat every two seconds for walking politely, ask him to sit when you stop. Reward him when he does. Soon your Maltese will sit calmly by your side whenever you stop to chat with friends. If you do not want your Maltese to sit automatically at every stop, make sure you say, "Sit" before you give him a treat.

PROBLEM BEHAVIORS

No dog is trouble free. They are complex creatures who have their own goals in life, some of which may not be in accord with your own. In some ways, a tiny dog like a Maltese can present even more problems than a larger one, mainly because people simply don't bother to train them. The result is a yippy, over-shy or over-aggressive spoiled brat.

The best way to handle dog problems is to understand that you and your dog may have differing views about what a problem is. For example, let's say you come home after work and find your dog has ripped up your shoes or a rug. You have a problem—a destructive dog. The dog also has a

Teaching "Sit" doesn't usually involve a little chair for your Maltese, but he might enjoy it!

problem—boredom and loneliness. When you understand that you have to fix his problem before your can fix yours, you are on the way to a well-behaved dog!

Also, some unpleasant behavior is normal. It is normal for dogs to bark (at least sometimes). It is normal for dogs to dig. It is normal for them to sniff each other's butts (and your crotch if only your Maltese could reach it). Some of this behavior can be redirected; the rest must be ignored or accepted.

Aggression (Dog-to-Dog)

Maltese are fine with being the only dog, and while two males can sometimes be hostile, the problem is usually solvable as long as you are the "pack leader" with all the family canines below you in status. It is sometimes, but not always true, that if you have several dogs, one will assume the position of alpha or dominant dog. Wolves always have a dominance hierarchy, but dogs are not wolves, even though they are grouped in the same genus. They don't behave in the same way, which is why most people don't keep wolves for pets.

To Jump or Not to Jump?

Opinions differ about the safety issues for jumping Maltese. These are fragile dogs and leaping from heights can be dangerous. On the other hand, Maltese are agile dogs who perform quite well in agility. In general, it's best not to let a Malty jump from heights greater than one foot (30.5 cm).

Dogs are social creatures, but sociability is connected, oddly enough, with squabbling. If dogs were truly non-social they would ignore each other. Instead, dogs form a "pack" and it often happens that there is a disagreement about who should head the pack. Hence the rumblings and sometimes outward fighting that is so abrasive to their owners. Most serious fighting occurs between fertile dogs of the same gender. In a normal household, fighting can occur when the previous "top dog" ages, or the younger dog suddenly "comes into his own," usually between the time is he is 18-months to 3-years-old. It's especially noticeable when one of the contenders has been absent for a period of time. In my house, the period of absence can be an hour. Although nerve-racking, this kind of squabbling is seldom serious, as long as you do not try to "make things right" by deciding who you think should be leader. Let the dogs sort it out for themselves. If you intervene, things can get worse and may last longer.

Solution

The solution in some cases is as simple as neutering the offending male. More commonly, the owner needs to take firm hold as a leader, and attempt to figure out what kinds of situations prompt the violence. If it's food, don't allow the dogs to eat near each other. Put them in separate rooms if you have to. If you give treats, give simple easy-to-swallow ones, not rawhide bones or other things that become "possessions." Some dogs fight when they enter enclosed spaces. In that case, teach your dogs to "wait" before allowing them to plunge out the door at the same time and start fighting. All dogs should know basic obedience.

Enhance the position of the naturally dominant dog by feeding, petting, greeting, and walking him first. The lower-ranked dog will soon figure out that he has no allies in his quest for leadership and will settle down into second place. You must do this even if you like the lower-status dog best. If there are frequent fights, make sure they are wearing a harness or some other suitable neckwear so that you can easily grab them. Don't stick your hand between fighting dogs. You know what will happen—even a tiny Maltese bite can make you bleed.

In extremely serious cases, you may have to separate the dogs, temporarily or permanently. In some cases, pharmaceutical intervention may help, but that should be a last resort.

Attention-Seeking Behavior

People-oriented dogs like Maltese adore attention, and some will go to almost any lengths to get it. At first it's cute and even flattering—later, however, it can become a real nuisance. Attention-seeking behavior ranges from a gentle but insistent nudge to loud barking and jumping in your face (never underestimate just how high a Malt can jump). Some paw at you. Some will steal anything you're holding. A few have been known to roll around on the floor, apparently in agony, to get you to pay attention to their feigned ailment.

Solution

Since your Malty is engaging in this behavior to get your attention, any kind of attention he gets for it (including negative attention) is a reward for him. To cure the problem, you'll have to consistently ignore him when he seeks attention. (However, be sure that you *do* give him attention when he is quiet and undemanding. Dogs do need attention; Maltese thrive on it.) This is harder than it seems, because at first the problem may get worse not better, as the dog intensifies his attempts to make you pay attention. He'll just figure that since his previous attempts had been unsuccessful, he just needs to try a little harder. After an undetermined period however, your intelligent Maltese will decide that his tactics no longer work.

Some behaviorists suggest using a so-called bridging device to hasten the progress. In this plan, whenever the dog engages in the unwanted behavior you blow a whistle or use some other signal to let the dog know in advance what you are about to do, which is leave the room. The bridging device helps focus the dog's attention on precisely what he's doing the second before you leave. This in turn leads to a quicker extinguishment of the behavior.

Sometimes there is disagreement over who should be "top dog" in the family.

Barking (Excessive)

Dogs bark. It's a normal part of their behavior. They bark to alert us to visitors, they bark in play, and they bark when they want something. It is not possible or desirable to eliminate all barking in our canine friends. However, sometime barking exceeds tolerable limits. In that case, it's called "nuisance barking."

Nuisance barking can be a serious problem in Maltese, but it almost always occurs in dogs who are left alone for long periods. Unlike terriers, Shelties, and many smaller breeds, the Maltese is not genetically "programmed" to be a barker, but a lonely situation can quickly turn him into one. And it is true that some Maltys seem to enjoy listening to themselves bark. This is sometimes known as recreational barking. The Maltese can be an "alarm" barker—letting you know when you have visitors of any species. This isn't a bad thing, after all you want the dog to do his job. The problem begins when you can't shut the alarm off or when the dog barks for another reason, such as to guard his territory or express his boredom and displeasure.

Solution

For the territorial barker, it may help to obscure the boundary beyond your house and your neighbor's by installing stockade-type fencing. Chain link allows the dog to see what's going on next door and pay far too much attention to it. If you hear him barking, bring him in immediately. That may be what he wants, anyway, and who can blame him? Standing around all by oneself in the backyard isn't that much fun. Most importantly, however, barking may annoy the neighbors, and you don't want that. In my hometown, a local science teacher was convicted of actually poisoning the dog next door because the dog's barking annoyed him. While I am quite sure your neighbors are not like this, you never really know.

Your Maltese may be barking because he's bored. The cure its simple (but not always easy)—exercise! Even the apartment-loving Maltese benefits form a good brisk run or game time. Tired dogs don't bark.

Closely related to the boredom barker is the neurotic barker. Boredom can lead to neurosis and separation anxiety. The cure again lies in more training, work, play, and sensible, disciplined

Be a Good Leader

Many times a household of squabbling dogs is a good indication that the owner is weak or ineffectual. A strong leader simply exudes an atmosphere in which no fighting is permissible. In a few cases, however, a dog who was not properly socialized as a puppy can continue to have aggression problems no matter how insightful the owner is. These animals simply need to be "only dogs."

treatment. In serious cases, medication may be needed, at least temporarily.

To minimize barking while you are gone, keep the dog in a quiet part of your home, draw the blinds (darkness is calming), and leave on the radio tuned to a talk station. This white noise masks other noises, and comforts your dog with the sound of a human voice.

Chewing

Dogs are natural chewers; it's part of their heritage. They will chew on rawhide, bones, shoes, toys, razor blades, and coat hangers. Bored dogs, left alone for hours at a time, chew even more. And dogs with separation anxiety, who are more frantic than bored, begin chewing the instant the owner leaves and continues throughout the day. He may only stop chewing to bark and whine. Maltese can get bored and lonely when deprived of your company. They don't know you are hard at work providing for their every need. They prefer your company to the finest accoutrements on earth.

Solution

The best way to stop inappropriate chewing is to keep your dog happy, partnered, and exercised. If you can't spend much time with your dog, hire someone who can, or take your dog to doggy day care.

You can help your Maltese entertain himself by providing him with a variety of interactive toys. Some of these can be stuffed with cheese, small treats, or peanut butter. Leave on the TV or radio to a talk station (they like that better than music).

The worst way to try and solve the problem is to confine the dog. While this will stop the chewing problem (for you), it will do nothing to relieve his tension or boredom. In fact, it will make it worse.

Digging

Maltese are natural diggers. For them dirt is a couch, a nesting

Some behavior problems are a sign of boredom or loneliness.

bed, a cooling-off spa, a hunting ground, and an escape route. It helps if you can figure out exactly what motivates your particular Maltese to dig, and then you can find the answers.

Solution

If he's looking for a soft spot, he'll head for your garden. To manage the behavior, you'll have to make the garden off-limits (fencing is a must), and supply a "digging box"—a sandbox made of soft earth for him to enjoy.

For over-heated dogs, a baby pool is a welcome addition. But when it's really hot, bring the dog in the house during those balmy 90°F (32°C) summer days. There are also "cooling blankets" that you might want to employ.

If he's trying to escape, he'll be digging near the fence line, you may have to reinforce the fence by pouring six inches of concrete underneath it.

Many people divide their yards into "people areas" and "dog areas" and separate them by a fence. This is a last resort, but it will work. If your dog makes a trail through your yard, don't try to replant over it, just turn it into a path.

Food Stealing

Maltese do not steal. It is beneath them. However, they will take advantage of an opportunity when it presents itself. Luckily, you have a Maltese, not a Mastiff.

Solution

The easiest way to keep your Maltese away from your food is simply put it out of reach, and really, that's not too hard. Some people say that if you keep your dog well fed, he won't be motivated to steal, to which I say stuff and nonsense. Mammals are programmed to be hungry pretty much all the time. Most dogs will eat themselves sick if they get a chance, although I must tell you most Maltese are more sensible than that. Still you never know, do you?

Inappropriate Elimination

Between 10 and 20 percent of dog behavior problems are categorized as "inappropriate elimination," a state of affairs in which your dog uses your house for his bathroom. This is to be expected in young puppies, of course, but when old dogs engage in the same behavior, we need to look further than the tiny bladder, weak sphincter muscles, and the ignorance of a puppy.

If your previously housetrained dog reverts to this behavior, you need to figure out what precipitated it. It is possible, for instance, that you simply have not been paying enough attention to his signals to go out, or that he is left alone too long to "hold it." (Put your self in his place. How long would you like to be left without access to a bathroom?) A dog that makes a mistake because he is left alone too long or that has given signals which you ignore does not have a problem—you do. This is something you need to handle by changing your schedule or by simply paying more attention.

Medical Causes

House soiling can have several medical causes, including: bladder infections or bladder stones, diabetes, Cushing's disease, canine cognitive dysfunction in geriatric dogs,

parasites, gastroenteritis, and problems with the pancreas. If your dog suddenly begins eliminating in the house, it's time for a veterinary check up.

Marking

Male dogs may also engage in "marking behavior," leaving a small amount of urine in strategic places around the house. This is most likely to occur when two or more males share a home. It's most common in unneutered males, but neutered dogs and in a few cases even females may wish to "compete" in this game. It is more common when a new dog comes to stay or visit. To correct this habit, you should make sure that the dogs know that *you* are the leader of the house and that marking *their* territory there is useless. Housetrain the dog as you would a new puppy, taking him outside when you catch him in the act, and cleaning any marked areas very thoroughly with a non-ammonia-based cleaner.

Submissive Urination

Nervous and unsure dogs sometimes

If your Maltese is a digger, you might want to divide your yard into a "dog area."

exhibit "submissive urination" when they are scolded or feel insecure. These dogs, even males, typically squat to urinate, although it tends to be more common in females. To correct the problem, try not to look at your dog any more than necessary. Let him come over to you, not vice versa. Be calm, and never punish or scold him for urinating—he is scared of something and can't help himself. In the wild, a submissive dog who urinates wins the approval of the higher-status pack mates, and he is hoping for the same response from you. Of course, you can't give it to him, since you want him to stop this behavior, but you can't punish him either as that will simply reinforce in his mind his inferior status and he will try harder (more urinating) to placate you. The best thing you can do is ignore the behavior and do things in general to boost his confidence.

If your dog engages in this behavior only when you are not home, you may have a dog with separation anxiety (see below).

Nipping and Play Biting

While some puppy biting is a teething behavior, in most

it's a form of social play. (Teething behavior is much more likely to be chewing than nipping.) The key is making your Maltese puppy understand what dog trainers call "bite inhibition." Most puppies learn it in the litter from their mother and littermates, one reason why taking home a puppy too early can lead to problems. Puppies learn valuable social skills from their littermates! Your job as owner is to give your dog plenty of opportunity for playing that does not involve nipping. Examples include fetch and retrieving games, swimming, or learning tricks. You can even buy chicken flavored soap bubbles that dogs like to chase! On the other hand, games like wrestling and tug o' war may encourage some dogs to bite or grab—it depends on the dog.

Solution

If your Malt tends to grab play bite, it's up to you to teach him that dog teeth don't belong on human hands. (Well-socialized, bite inhibited dogs, on the other hand, enjoy gently taking your hand in their mouths and leading you around.) To help your dog understand this lesson, send out a pained "yelp" when he tries to nip you. If possible do not pull away your hand—that encourages him to bite down harder. He thinks it's a game. Instead, you want him to remove his mouth. Most of the time, a sharp yelp lets the puppy know he has made a mistake. However, you need to be consistent about this—it doesn't work to let the puppy play bite sometimes and not others. Don't use punishment to stop this behavior—the chances are that it will only increase aggression. Remember that your puppy is trying to play with you, he just doesn't know how yet.

If your Maltese gets overly excited and starts to play bite, you can also try a short (30 seconds to 2 minute) "time out." Leave the room—without the dog. He'll quickly figure out that nipping results in the end of play and learn to inhibit his bite.

Too Excited

Some dogs urinate when they are very excited, but this behavior is more typical of young puppies who just can't hold it. Just ignore the behavior and the dog will soon outgrow it when his sphincter muscles get stronger.

Self-mutilation

Self-mutilation, such as acral lick dermatitis, occurs when dogs lick or bite themselves excessively. You will see hair loss, sores, or rashes on the affected part of the body. The causes may be medical or psychological.

Solution

If the cause is medical, the condition will usually resolve once the underlying condition is treated, although it can happen that the behavior may stay even after the medical problem is addressed. For instance, acral lick granuloma may begin as a simple flea bite or infection but progresses to an obsession in which the dog cannot leave the foot alone. This is considered an obsessive-compulsive disorder. Other factors that may lead to it are anxiety, stress caused by long periods of confinement, isolation, harassment from another pet, or repeated exposure to scary noises. Your vet will do a physical exam and perhaps take a skin scraping or allergy testing. He may ask for a blood test or chemistry profile, and may prescribe a treatment to relieve the itch. If medical causes are ruled out, he will recommend you do your best to remove the stressors in the dog's life. In some cases anti-obsession medication like serotonin reuptake inhibitors may be recommended.

Separation Anxiety

Canine separation anxiety (SA) is a behavioral disorder characterized by a dog who panics or becomes terribly upset and nervous when left alone. Such dogs are pathologically attached to their owners. SA dogs are destructive and may attempt to flee the home—some dogs have been known to go through windows! This behavior is a mark of a dog's fear, not some attempt to "get back at" or take revenge on his owners, although it may seem like that. Maltese are extremely prone to this disorder (more than many other breeds) as they were bred to be deeply dependent upon humans for their well-being and happiness.

Dogs who typically exhibit separation anxiety share several of these characteristics:

- Acquired by the owner after three months of age or before six weeks of age
- Orphaned or hand-raised
- Acquired from a shelter
- Had several different homes/owners

If your Maltese starts eliminating inappropriately, have him checked by a vet.

Dog with separation anxiety are often "Velcro" dogs while you are home, following you about everywhere. They become anxious at signs of your leaving, and begin to whine and cry almost immediately (and without ceasing) when you do go. They may yip in a high-pitched tone, defecate or urinate in the home, destroy property, and refuse to eat in your absence. (These behaviors begin within 30 minutes after you leave.) If the dog displays these behaviors while you are home, he probably does not have separation anxiety. In addition, a dog with separation anxiety becomes overly enthusiastic upon your return.

Solution

There is no easy solution to separation anxiety, but there is some training and behavior work you can do to try and help desensitize your dog to your leaving.

- Rehearse your leaving. First, imitate your daily departure routine, including all the prep work.
- Give your dog a very special, high-value treat that he gets only while you are absent from the home—something stuffed with good cheese or even meat.
- Don't make a big, anxious deal about leaving. Just say,"Good-

bye, Silver," and take off. Come back in 15 seconds—before he knows what hit him. Praise him if he has been quiet and non-destructive.

- Then leave again. Continue until the dog stops barking. Over a period of weeks you can leave for longer and longer periods of time. Don't try to do this too fast—expect it to take a long time.
- Never punish a dog for having separation anxiety. That will only make it worse.
- You can also encourage independent play in your Maltese by providing him with interesting toys that do not require human interaction.

At present, clomipramine (used once or twice a day) is the only FDA-approved drug for the treatment of separation anxiety in dogs. However, some other human anti-anxiety medications have also been used. Drugs are meant to be used as a supplement to training, however, not instead of training.

Thunderphobia

Dog who fear thunderstorms (or other loud noises) may seek your attention, hide behind the toilet, or try to run away. Don't reassure your dog during a fearful event with petting, soothing words, or extra attention—that merely confirms his suspicion that something is really wrong. Redirect your Maltese by being happy and focused on something else. In mild cases you can turn on the radio, or just let the dog hide. Many people have found that plug-in or spray "dog appeasing pheromones" are very helpful; they can be found in pet-supply stores. Your Maltese's veterinarian or veterinary behaviorist may also recommend anti-anxiety medication.

HOW TO FIND AN ANIMAL BEHAVIOR CONSULTANT

For some recalcitrant problems you may need professional help—help that goes beyond what a regular dog trainer can offer you. A behaviorist is trained to help you deal with abnormal behaviors as well as the usual ones. A veterinary behaviorist is probably top of the line, because they can prescribe needed medications as well as help you understand the dog's emotional problems; however, there aren't many of them in the country! Another choice is a certified applied animal behaviorist. Most of these people have a Ph.D. in Animal Behavior, but unfortunately not all of them specialize in companion animals. Your best bet is probably to discuss your options with your vet. And that's convenient, because that's where you are going first.

Puppies need to chew, so give your Maltese plenty of chew toys.

Yes, the first thing you need to do is to have your dog examined by a veterinarian to make sure there is no medical problem underlying the odd behavior. One study showed that more than 20 percent of dogs who were brought into the vet for a behavioral consultation and who had not seen a vet in six months had a contributing health issue.

Once your Maltese has been checked over and found healthy, get at least two referrals from your vet. Call each consultant and hold nothing back in describing the problem. Be honest. A good behaviorist should listen to you carefully, not just demand you make an appointment. A good behaviorist knows that the owner is likely to be part of the problem and will be especially interested in the family dynamic.

Ask questions yourself, such as how long an appointment usually lasts, how many appointments might be needed, and what happens during the appointment. A good therapist does not promise miracles, does not hide costs, and is willing to care about your dog as much as you do. Remember, there is a solution for almost any behavioral problem, if you look hard enough.

7

ADVANCED TRAINING AND ACTIVITIES

With Your Maltese

Believe it or not, your Maltese is more than lap candy! He is a small white wizard who can accomplish magic, if you'll just take the time to teach him the ropes (after you learn them yourself, of course).

AGILITY

This sport has taken the dog world by storm! Agility first made an appearance at the famous UK Crufts Dog Show in 1978, and it is currently the fastest growing dog sport in the United States. And, your dog doesn't have to be Mr. Universe to complete well in agility trials.

Agility is a timed course over obstacles. The agility dog needs to be able to run full speed for a number of minutes, turn, twist, climb, jump, and dart through tunnels. Many of the obstacles have "contact" zones that require the dog to actually put his feet down in certain places—this prevents dangerous "fly-offs" where the dog could become injured. Here the handler runs the dog through and over a variety of obstacles including jumps, chutes, tunnels, weave poles, ramps, and seesaws. In serious competition, classes are divided by height. Kennel clubs also offer classes in agility, and if you are handy with a hammer and saw, you can even make your own agility equipment from PVC pipes, plywood, and children's tunnels.

Maltese are more athletic than they appear, and if yours obeys simple commands, he may be a natural for this sport!

The AKC has its own agility competition, limited to registered dogs with pedigrees (or ILPs); other organizations offer agility to any and all breeds. Dogs must be one year old to compete. Since the jumps are adjusted according to the height of the dog, a small, agile dog can compete very well in agility events. The title your dog can earn are: Novice Agility (NA); Open Agility

Agility is a fun and fast-growing dog sport.

(OA); Agility Excellent (AX); Master Agility Excellent (MX). Other tiles include Jumpers with Weaves Novice (NAJ), Open (OAJ) and Excellent (MXJ). The supreme tile in agility is Master Agility Champion (MACH).

To learn more about this wonderful sport, check out the United States Dog Agility Association (www.usdaa.com) and the North American Dog Agility Council (www.nadac.com). The American Kennel Club (www.akc.org), the United Kennel Club (www.ukcdogs.com), and the Kennel Club UK (www.the-kennel-club.org.uk) also offer agility competitions. All these organization schedule events, keep track of "points," and award titles.

CAMPING

Nothing beats sleeping under the stars with your faithful friend snoozing peacefully at your side. Don't count on the Maltese to protect you, however. In bear country, dogs can actually attract bears who are looking for a late night snack, and even the fiercest Maltese on earth cannot handle a grizzly by

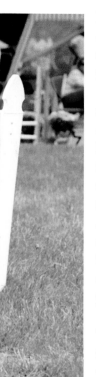

himself (or really even a grouchy raccoon). They are also curious creatures who may run afoul of a skunk, an event which could end your camping trip fairly quickly.

Of course it's important to check ahead to make sure the campground allows dogs, and under what conditions. Most require dogs to be kept on a lead, but policies can change from year to year. It's important to take some safety precautions. Campfire can be fatally attractive to dogs, especially if they are redolent with the smell of cooking hotdogs. Ashes remain hot for hours, so monitor your dog at all times. If your dog will be swimming, check out the currents and provide your dog with a flotation device. And be considerate of others—pick up the poop, and don't allow your dog to bark or wander.

Pack for the weather, and expect the unexpected. Thunderstorms, high winds, and blizzards can come seemingly out of nowhere. A jacket for your Malty will be appreciated in cold weather. Also, carry a recent picture of your dog. It's not enough to say you've lost your Maltese. Believe it or not, many people don't know a Maltese from a millipede.

Your camping partner should be up to date on vaccinations, including Lyme disease if you are entering a tick-infested area, which is practically anywhere in the woods. And of course he should carry plenty of identification. Bring insect repellent and be sure your dog is on a tick, flea and heartworm prevention program.

Since you'll be bringing a first aid kit for yourself, include antibiotic ointment, Vetrap (an elastic bandage that sticks only to itself and can hold bandages in places without pins or adhesive tapes), and Benadryl for bee stings.

Of course you'll carry in adequate food and water for your dog, and pack everything up in a bear-proof container—just in case. You shouldn't be in bear country with a dog, but just in case…

At night, bring your dog into the tent with you. You'll both feel safer and you can keep each other warm. And when you leave your cozy campsite—clean up—being sure to check

Sports and Safety

All dogs engaged in sports are more subject to injury than the average pet. Before embarking on any canine sport, get your dog a compete veterinary checkup, start slow, and join an organization that will mentor you through the process. Your local kennel club is a good place to start.

around for dog waste. If you found the campsite lovely, others might too. Don't ruin it for them.

CANINE FREESTYLE (MUSICAL FREESTYLE, FREESTYLE DANCE)

This contemporary dog sport includes elements of obedience, dancing, and tricks—all set to music. In one form, called Freestyle Heeling, the dog is judged by his ability to maintain the heel position while the handler moves to music; the dog should appear invisibly tethered to his partner. In Musical Freestyle the dog performs a variety of tricks and is not required to keep "heeling." Popular moves include leg weaving, sending the dog away, moving together at a distance, jumps, spins, bows, rolling over, and dancing in partnership.

Currently, there are several organization regulating competitive freestyle, such as the World Canine Freestyle Organization (www.worldcaninefreestyle.org; canine Freestyle GB (www.caninefreestylegb.com); and Canine Freestyle Federation (www.canine-freestyle.org).

Competition rules vary from group to group, and from country to country, but most are based on a variety of technical and artistic merit points. Regardless of the style of routine to be

performed, all routines are done free of training aids or leashes (except in some beginner categories). Competition can be done as a single dog-and-handler team, as a pair of dogs and handlers, or as a full team of three or more dogs and their handlers.

The great thing about this sport is that you don't have to be very much of a dancer yourself.

Your Maltese can be a great camping buddy as long as you take some precautions.

The Canine Good Citizen Test recognizes well-trained dogs.

CANINE GOOD CITIZEN

The Canine Good Citizen (CGC) Test is your first step towards formal recognition for your wonderful, socialized, well-trained Maltese. Started in 1989, CGC is a certification program designed to reward dogs who show good manners in their community. It not only lays the basic foundation for more advanced work in performance events, but also gives your pet the basic skills he needs to negotiate 21st century life successfully.

Unlike some other formal events, spayed and neutered dogs are welcome, as well as mixed breeds. There is no age limit, but your dog must be old enough to have received immunizations and rabies vaccine. You'll need a leash and collar and a brush or comb for grooming.

The test consists of ten steps; dogs who pass it will receive a very nice, framable certificate from the American Kennel Club. The tests include:

- Test 1: Accepting a friendly stranger
- Test 2: Sitting politely for petting
- Test 3: Appearance and grooming
- Test 4: Out for a walk (walking on a loose lead)
- Test 5: Walking through a crowd

- Test 6: "Sit" and "down" on command and staying in place
- Test 7: Coming when called
- Test 8: Reaction to another dog
- Test 9: Reaction to distraction
- Test 10: Supervised separation

Show Etiquette

It's fun to go to a show just to look around. Don't bring your own dog to the show, however, unless he is entered. Most shows have a rule against this practice, since space is limited.

One of the great things about this event is that it allows everyone to go home a winner—you're not competing against other dogs, but simply attempting to fulfill the "passing requirements." This is a great opportunity to educate, bond, and have fun with your dog. You'll both benefit!

The Kennel Club has a similar program called The Kennel Club Good Citizen Dog Scheme, which is the largest dog training scheme in the UK.

DOG SHOWS (CONFORMATION)

When dog fanciers use the word "dog show," they are usually referring to conformation shows, or beauty contests, as some people like to think of them. The avowed purpose of

Even if your Maltese is not a show dog, he'll still be a winner in your eyes.

conformation shows is to identify those dogs who most closely resemble the breed standard and who are worthy to pass along their genes to the next generation. Therefore, only non-sterilized animals are allowed to compete. Dog shows pop up all around the country every weekend. It's a great opportunity to meet people, exhibit your dog, buy great dog stuff you can't get anywhere else, and learn a lot about dogs.

How Dog Shows Work

The first great object of showing a dog is to have your dog win the Champion title. Each breed competes separately towards that goal. (So your Maltese won't have to compete against a Poodle.) To do that, you would enter at the "class level"—either in Puppy, Novice, American Bred, Bred By Exhibitor, or the Open class. In each class, four ribbons are awarded, but only the winner goes to the Winners' class. Up through this point, males (dogs) and females (bitches) compete separately. All of these first place dogs from all the previous classes compete. The winner is named the Winners Dog or the Winners Bitch. These two Winners are the only dogs to earn points toward a Championship.

The number of points available ranges from one to five, depending on how many Maltese were entered in all of the classes. A win of three, four, or five points at a single show is called a "major." A dog must win at least two majors and earn a total of 15 points to become a Champion.

The Winners Dog and Winners Bitch then compete against each other for Best of Winners, as well as against any dogs who have already earned their Championships and are entered as "specials" for the Best of Breed. The Maltese named Best of Breed is then allowed to compete against other Toy Dog breeds for Best of Group. The Winner of the Group Competition faces other group winners for Best in Show.

What Happens in the Ring

While dogs don't have to do tricks to win at a conformation show, they need to show basic good

Matches

If you and your dog are still learning, it's fun to enter a "match" rather than a show. Matches are informal affairs, and you can enter the very day of the event. They are specifically designed for new handlers and novice dogs, so it's a great way to learn the ropes. You won't receive any "points" for winning, however, even if your dog turns out to be Best in Match.

Your show dog will have to learn how to be "stacked" to show him off at his best advantage.

manners. Your dog will need to get used to having a stranger check him out—including teeth, and in the cases of males, testicles. Make sure your Maltese leaves other dogs strictly alone—no sniffing or socializing allowed. It's just possible an untoward disagreement might occur, and I have seen large dogs urinating on smaller ones, a very unfortunate event for a show dog (especially the one on the bottom).

A dog is judged both standing and trotting ("gaiting") around the ring. The dog is moved in straight lines, circles, and triangles, with you or the handler at the end of the lead. When standing, you may decide to "stack your dog," or you may decide to "free bait" him. In a stack, the dog is held by the handler, with one hand on the neck and the other on the tail (usually holding it up). In a free bait, the handler stands away from the dog and the dog stands at attention. This is more natural and beautiful, but not enough people work at getting that wonderful response!

Some people show (or handle) their own dogs, others hire a professional. But before you actually step into the ring, take some handling classes at your local kennel club, and go to a few dog shows. Handling classes can be invaluable. You'll learn dog show protocol, dress, and terminology, and how to gait and pose your dog.

If you are interested in this sport, get a mentor, preferably someone from your local Maltese or kennel club, to help you out.

HIDE AND SEEK

You don't have to exhaust yourself and your Maltese by tearing around in the dog park to have a good time. That's one of the beauties of the breed—you can play games right at home. Try hide 'n seek. Toss a treat into the next room and while your dog has scampered along after it, take the opportunity to hide somewhere quickly. When your Maltese finds you, reward him with another small treat. Or you can try hiding the treat itself. Make it simple at first, like hiding it in one hand and then the other—asking your Malt to "guess the hand." Later you can try hiding the treat somewhere in the living room. Then when you've had enough of that, it's time to sit back and read some Jane Austen together.

Fun for Kids

Even kids can compete in events designed to display their dog-handling skills in Junior Showmanship classes.

OBEDIENCE

When begun in 1933, AKC obedience trials were designed to foster training and demonstrate a dog's willingness to work closely with people. Today, obedience trials are held at most all-breed dog shows. Obedience trials are open to all recognized breeds, and the tiny Maltese excels in the obedience ring. In fact,

Competing may not be for you—teaching your Maltese some fun tricks can be just as rewarding.

the ideal obedience dog needs to have many of the same characteristics as a show dog. Like a good conformation dog, an obedience dog needs to have good structure, good movement, and an attentive personality. Shy, overly submissive, or dominant dogs have temperament problems that make them less suitable for this demanding sport.

The Westminster Dog Show

Next to the Kentucky Derby, the Westminster Dog show is the oldest, continuous sporting event held in the United States. The original "Westminster" was actually a bar in a hotel of the same name. (The hotel no longer exists.) The first members of the club were men who owned gun dogs, and even today the logo of the show is a representation of Sensation, a pointer owned by one of the members, who had a legendary ability to point birds. In 1877, the club held its first dog show, called the "First Annual New York Bench Show of Dogs." Since 1883 it has been held in Madison Square Garden. So far, a Maltese has not attained the title "Best in Show," but there's always next year.

Your Maltese can win various obedience degrees. To attain the first of these "degrees," the CD or Companion Dog Title, a dog must heel on leash, heel free, stand for examination, recall, and complete a long sit (60 seconds) and a long down (3 minutes). When heeling, he has to execute left and right turns, stops, and move at various speeds. On the "stand," he needs to stand still off lead while a judge examines him. The handler must be at least 6 feet (1.8 m) away. The recall requires the dog to sit 30 feet (9 m) from the handler, come quickly, and then sit. On command, the dog moves to the heel position and sits once more.

Earning a CDX title (Companion Dog Excellent) requires your dog to work entirely off lead. He has to heel off lead in a figure eight pattern, drop on recall (going "down" rather than just sitting), retrieve a dumbbell from 20 feet (6 m) over level ground, retrieve a dumbbell over the high jump, and jump the broad jump. He must also do longer sits (3 minutes) and downs (5 minutes) with the handler completely out of sight.

The highest degree is Utility. Utility dogs must follow hand signals for heeling, moving, and standing for examination. The handler cannot use voice signals in this section. Dogs also participate in directed jumping, directed retrieve, and scent discrimination. Dogs can work for their Utility and CDX degrees at the same time.

Rally Obedience

This fast-paced sport is more fun and dog-friendly than traditional obedience and offers four title levels for your dog. In rally obedience, you can talk or even sing to your dog, which is not permitted in regular obedience. Unlike in regular obedience, your dog isn't required to have a picture-perfect heel, and there is a lot more variety than in regular obedience. A qualifying score is 70 out of 100 possible points.

TRACKING

Tracking is formally part of obedience, but is really a separate event. A dog work towards his Tracking Dog (TD) title by following a human scent laid from 30 minutes to 2 hours before the trial. The track is from 440 to 500 yards (402 to 457 m) long and includes turns. The Tracking Dog Excellent (TDX) title is

Obedience Training

Training for obedience begins with fun and games that teach the dog to focus on his owner. The more time and human interaction the dog gets when young, the more suitable a candidate he'll be for obedience work later on.

Their sweet nature and lovable temperaments make Maltese excellent therapy dogs.

earned by following an older (3 to 5 hours) and longer track with more turns and more obstacles.

Another tracking title is the Variable Surface Tracking (VST) title in which a dog tackles the urban jungle, walking down streets, up stairs and other vegetation-bare areas. This track is between 3 to 5 hours old.

THERAPY

Dogs are natural born healers of both the body and the spirit. By now, most people are familiar with the idea of owners and their pets taking part in a regular visitation program of hospitals, children's homes, psychiatric institutions, assisted-care facilities, and even prisons! Many persons, no matter what their age, health, or status in society may be benefit from having close contact with animals. In fact there's even a name for this activity—Animal Assisted Therapy (AAT).

Maltese make wonderful therapy dogs. They are infinitely strokeable, and small enough to sit quietly on the smallest and frailest of laps. They can also be easily picked up and carried to a bedside or out the way of busy hospital traffic. In addition, while German Shepherds or Rottweilers make excellent therapy dogs, many people may have negative associations with such breeds. The sweet Maltese, on the other hand, evokes a positive response from nearly everyone.

To participate in Animal Assisted Therapy, it's best to have your pet certified, either by the facility where you'll be volunteering or by a national pet therapy organization or its affiliate. In some cases, you'll just be making the rounds, visiting, and talking with residents (many of whom have literally no one else to talk to). In other cases your pet will be part of a specific treatment plan, with clear goals set forth

on each visit.

Certification programs vary, but many require that your dog complete a full obedience course, a health screen, and be of a minimum age (usually one year). Of course, a good therapy dog should be bathed and groomed (especially the nails), and be free of fleas. You certainly wouldn't want your Maltese causing a flea infestation at the local hospital! As far as personality goes, two qualities are of the essence: friendliness and obedience. A dog who is just one or the other is not suitable. A mean or excessively shy dog is obviously not the best choice for therapy. And no matter how friendly, an out-of-control Maltese in a hospital or nursing home does a lot more harm than good.

Even well-behaved therapy dogs aren't for everyone, however. Patients in intensive care, those who have compromised immune systems, serious allergies, or are fearful of dogs (or just don't like them) are not good candidates for this type of therapy. And of course, people who lack self-control or who have a record of sudden violence should not be allowed contact with pets.

If you decide that AAT is for you, make sure that you can plan to devote a certain amount of time to it each week or month. People come to expect and look forward to regular visits, and they often form close attachments to your dog. (And I think the dog enjoys the visits just as much.) It isn't fair to anyone to make a half-hearted or sporadic commitment. You are dealing with people's hearts and feelings. Remember that your visits can make just as much a difference in people's lives as medicine and good food.

The Benefits of Therapy Dogs

The American Heart Association has documented that therapeutic dogs lower anxiety, stress, and heart and lung pressure among heart failure patients. In fact, therapy dogs seem to best their human companions. In one study, anxiety (measured by a standard rating scale) dropped 24 percent for those visited by the dog and volunteer team, but only by 10 percent for those visited by just a human volunteer. The scores for the group with no visit remained the same. Even more interesting, levels of epinephrine, a hormone the body makes when stressed, dropped about 17 percent in patients visited by a person and a dog, and 2 percent in those visited just by a person. Levels rose about 7 percent in the group that didn't get visitors.

HEALTH
of Your Maltese

Nothing is more important to a responsible dog owner than the health of his or her dog, and in this case, nature and good breeding have given you a head start, for on the whole the Maltese is a healthy breed with fewer inherited problems than most breeds.

One thing you can do to ensure your Malty's continued good health is to find a veterinarian you trust, and to take your dog in for annual checkups.

CHOOSING A VETERINARIAN

Your veterinarian is your Maltese's best friend. Start looking for a veterinarian before you bring your Maltese home. You don't want to search around *after* your dog becomes sick or has a problem. Remember that most animal illnesses require professional care. If you delay a trip to the vet, you not only risk your dog's life, but add to the eventual cost. To find a good veterinarian, ask friends, your breeder, or your local kennel club for recommendations.

What to Look For

When you find a veterinarian you think might be right for your Maltese, go ahead and check the

Distance Matters

A few minutes difference in driving time can make the difference between life and death in case of poisoning or accidents. Check to find the nearest veterinary emergency clinic, and keep a map of how to get there on your fridge and in the glove compartment of your car.

facility out. Don't be afraid to ask for a tour. Consider the following on your visit:

- Is the staff relaxed, friendly, and compassionate?
- Is the veterinarian familiar with Maltese and their special needs?
- What other services do they provide? Boarding? Grooming? Home visits? Twenty-four hour emergency care?
- Are any of the staff specialists in orthopedics, holistic treatments, behavior, or cardiology?
- What hours is the clinic open? Evenings? Weekends? Who answers the calls when the office is closed? (If you work days, you should choose a clinic with evening hours.)
- How close is the office to your home? A difference of five minutes can mean life or death.
- Does the clinic accept pet insurance?
- Is the clinic a member of a spay/neuter program?
- How many Maltese does the clinic handle? How familiar are the staff with the Maltese's special health concerns?

Adding up the answers to all these questions may make it easier to decide on the right vet for you.

EXAMS

Preventive care for your Maltese is essential for his health. You should visit your veterinarian several times with your Maltese puppy, and then yearly once he's an adult.

You should visit your veterinarian several times with your Maltese puppy.

Puppy's First Exam

You should schedule your puppy's first visit to the vet as soon as possible after you get him. If you are a new dog owner, or at least new to the vet, you'll be asked to fill out some paperwork about you and your Malty. Usually a veterinary technician will weigh your puppy, take his temperature, listen to his heart, and perhaps get a fecal sample to check for worms. The vet will then chat with you about your puppy's general condition and health. The physical exam will include checking the puppy's eyes, ears, teeth, and skin. The vet will check the navel for hernia, the abdomen for pain, and listen to the heart and lungs for abnormal sounds. He or she will move the legs to check the knee caps to make sure they are not too lose (a special problem for the Maltese). The vet will also check the genitals and talk about future spaying or neutering. A vaccination protocol will be discussed. This would be the time for you to bring up any special concerns you may have.

Annual Exams

Most people take their dogs in for an annual checkup, but it would be wise to make this a twice-a-year appointment. Dogs age faster than we do and early detection of problems is the best way to avoid serious illnesses and big bills later. Talk to your vet about scheduling regular appointments.

VACCINATIONS

Vaccinations save lives. Before the days of effective veterinary vaccines, dogs were victims of canine distemper, hepatitis, and rabies. Now these diseases are rare. When parvo first emerged on the scene in the late 1970s innumerable dogs died, until a vaccine was developed. While there is an ongoing discussion about how

Vaccinations have saved the lives of millions of dogs.

often and against what dogs need to be vaccinated, make no mistake—you owe it to your Maltese and your community to get your pet vaccinated. While some people have healthy pets without their ever vaccinating them, they are relying mostly on the good sense of their neighbors, who get *their* pets vaccinated and thus have reduced the possibility of transmission.

Consult with your veterinarian about his or her vaccine protocol, and don't be afraid to ask questions.

Diseases to Vaccinate Against

Although vaccination protocols differ from place to place, and even from vet to vet, your puppy should be vaccinated against some or all of the following diseases.

Bordetella

Bordetella, also know as "kennel cough," can be caused by many organisms. It is similar to a bad cold in older dogs, but can be serious in puppies. True to its name, dogs with Bordetella cough, wheeze, hack, and sneeze. Bordetella vaccines are important if your dog will be visiting a lot of other dogs or housed in a kennel. The vaccine commonly given for kennel cough, however, does not protect against all forms of the disease. No cure exists—only supportive treatment, and in some cases antibiotics.

Coronavirus

Coronavirus is a disease related to the human cold, and is most serious in puppies. Coronavirus is passed through contaminated feces of an infected dog. It is very contagious and produces vomiting, diarrhea, and depression, symptoms similar to those of parvovirus. This vaccine is only recommended in areas where coronavirus is rampant.

Distemper

Distemper is the main killer of dogs worldwide. It destroys the nervous system, and attacks every tissue in the body. It is caused by an airborne, measles-like virus. The incubation period is 7 to 21 days, and initial symptoms include lethargy, fever, runny nose, diarrhea and yellow discharge from the eyes. The dog shows labored breathing, and loses his appetite. Later symptoms include a nervous twitch and thickening of the pads and nose, which is why the disease was once known as "hardpad." Dogs who progress to this stage are unlikely to make a complete recovery.

Hepatitis

Hepatitis, a serious disease caused by an adenovirus, is most dangerous in puppies. It is spread by contact with an infected dog, or with his urine or feces. The white blood cell count drops and some dogs experience clotting problems. It also affects the kidneys and liver. Symptoms include high fever, red mucus membranes, depression, and loss of appetite. Small blood spots may appear on the gums, and the eyes look bluish. Even dogs who recover often experience chronic illnesses; they may also shed the virus for months, infecting others. Luckily, this disease is seldom seen nowadays, largely because of the effective vaccines against it.

Leptospirosis

Leptospirosis is a worldwide bacterial infection that can be passed on to human beings. Dogs can contract this disease through exposure to the urine of an infected dog, rat, or wildlife. Leptospirosis affects the liver and kidney, and, in its most dangerous form, can even cause kidney failure. Even if the dog survives the disease, he can have permanent kidney damage. Treatment includes antibiotics and supportive care. An immunization is available for some forms of leptospirosis; however, many vets do not recommend its use, especially for young puppies. The "older" forms of leptospirosis are seldom seen nowadays, and the shot can cause reactions in some dogs. Recently, the disease has returned in a new and virulent strain, one that was previously seen only in horses and cows. An immunization against this "new" leptospirosis strain is being tested.

Lyme Disease

Lyme disease, carried primarily by the deer tick, was first identified in Old Lyme Connecticut, during the 1970s. It is now endemic in most of the US, especially in the northeast. The incubation period is from two to five months. It causes acute,

Good to Know

Though not always standard, in some cases your Maltese may require vaccinations against coronavirus, Lyme disease, and giardia. Check with your veterinarian.

You may be tempted to try and vaccinate your puppy yourself, but that's better left to the professionals.

intermittent lameness and fever as well as heart and kidney disease. If untreated, your dog can have permanent arthritis. It's advisable to give your dog this vaccine if you live in an endemic area and your dog spends a lot of time traipsing around in the woods (probably not likely for your Maltese, but you never know).

Parvovirus

Parvovirus, a highly contagious, deadly virus first appeared in 1978. It is transmitted through the feces of infected dogs. This virus invades and destroys rapidly growing cells in the intestine, bone marrow and lymphoid tissue and even the heart muscles, resulting in nausea, depression, vomiting, and severe bloody diarrhea. The disease can vary from mild to fatal, especially in puppies, if not properly treated. To make matters worse, parvo is a cold-hardy virus which can survive in infected feces at temperatures as low as 20°F (-7°C).

Rabies

Rabies is a deadly neurological viral disease transmitted through the bite of an infected animal. Getting a rabies vaccination for your dog is not only safe and sensible, it is mandatory everywhere in the United States. Puppies should be immunized against this disease at between 16 and 24 weeks of age.

Vaccination Protocols

While vaccination scheduling is a matter or controversy (and is constantly changing), here are the current recommendations for most dogs.

Puppies (4 to 20 Weeks)

The vaccination series begins between 6 and 8 weeks of age. Typically the last vaccination is given between 14 and 16 weeks of age. These early vaccines should protect against canine distemper virus, canine adenovirus, parainfluenza, and canine parvovirus. In cases where your dog is exposed to others in closed area, a vaccine against bordetella is recommended. Rabies vaccine should be given in accordance with individual state laws usually between 16 and 26 weeks of age. Newer vaccines effective against specific forms of the leptospirosis are given in certain affected areas.

Good to Know

In the US, vaccinating for rabies is a special case since it is so deadly and is transmittable to people. You must vaccinate your dog according to local regulations. Some places this means yearly, other places once every three years.

Dogs (20 Weeks to 2 Years)

Young adults need booster shots (to ensure lifelong immunity) against the same diseases for which he was vaccinated as a puppy.

Dogs Over 2 Years

If your dog has had his puppy shots and boosters, you and your vet may wish to forgo further vaccination for three or four years. It is increasingly recognized that annual vaccinations are not necessary—although annual checkups certainly are!

Senior Dog

There are basically two camps of opinion about vaccinating older animals. Some say that older dogs (about age ten for your Maltese) have a weakened immune system and need more frequent vaccinations. Others maintain that older dogs have built up a sufficient body of immunization through their regular vaccines and need fewer (or no) vaccinations. Discuss these options with your vet.

THE VALUE OF SPAYING AND NEUTERING

Sterilizing your Maltese is the most responsible option as a pet owner. Over 12 million former pets are put to death every year because they are no longer wanted. Rather than producing more puppies, try adopting one of these needy animals instead.

But neutering your Maltese is not just about cutting down on

Spay or neuter your Maltese—it's the best thing for his health.

A Matter of Terminology

The word "neuter" applies to both male and female dogs, not just males, as some people seem to think. "Spay or neuter" is redundant. If you want to be gender-correct, it's "spay" or "ovohysterectemy" for a female, and "castrate" for a male. "Neuter" is correct for either sex. In the cat world, they use "alter."

the unwanted pet population. Neutering can help protect your dog from several reproductive related health problems, including mammary or testicular cancer, as well as pyometra, a deadly infection of the uterus. Spaying or neutering your dog before the age of six months can protect your Maltese against breast, ovarian, or prostate cancer. In fact, unspayed females are at an extremely high risk for mammary tumors, about 50 percent of which will be malignant.

Spaying and neutering also ensures that your Maltese will be spared the danger of whelping—having puppies is dangerous. Breeding correctly is also very expensive, requiring genetic testing and frequent examinations of mother and puppies. Can you afford several hundred dollars in the unlikely hope of making a profit later? And if the genetic tests turn out unfavorably, will you forgo breeding? Dogs with a history of, or first degree relatives with, diabetes, allergies, hip dysplasia, cancer, and the like should not be bred.

EXTERNAL PARASITES

Parasites cause problems that run the gamut from mild itching

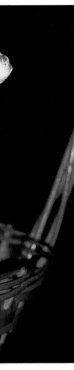

to death. External parasites include mites (sarcoptic, demodex, ear, or cheyletiella), fleas, and ticks. Many of these can be prevented or kept under control by preventive medications.

Fleas

There are over 2,200 species of fleas worldwide, but fortunately most of them live elsewhere than on your Maltese. The most common flea to attack dogs is the cat flea (*Ctenocephalides felis*). It can lay 50 eggs a day for 100 days—you do the math. (I was never very good at it, but 100 times 50 seems on the face of it to be an awful lot of fleas.) The smooth tiny eggs usually fall onto the carpet or into the couch. A few days later they hatch out into larvae. The larvae live largely on flea feces (a model of re-cycling, isn't it?). About a week later, the larvae spin themselves neat little cocoons and sleep away for a variable period of time, usually a couple of weeks, but occasionally several months.

Did You Know?

One great reason to live in high places—fleas can't stand altitude, although they don't mind heat or cold.

Thanks to modern science, these blood-sucking parasites aren't the problem they used to be. This is so true that I can tell you unreservedly that there is no reason for any modern dog to be afflicted with them. But it still happens, and even one flea is enough to cause a sensitive dog to develop flea allergy dermatitis. This painful, itchy condition is caused by certain enzymes in flea saliva. Once the dog starts scratching at the spot, he can get hot spots, hair loss, and secondary seborrhea. In many dogs, the condition becomes chronic.

We used to handle fleas by using sprays, powders, dips, and collars. And while some people still resort to these old-fashioned methods, most up-to-date owners choose to control fleas by capsule or use a spot-on liquid applied to the skin between the shoulder blades. More holistic owners rely on various combinations of herbs, although these are more effective as repellents than killers. But you really want to kill fleas, not repel them, since they might decide to take a bite out of you or some other hapless dog. Some products, like Frontline or Advantage, are available from your veterinarian, although you can get others at the pet supply or grocery store.

There are special shampoos that can help get rid of many external parasites.

Lice

Lice (*Trichodectes canis*) are a variety of chewing louse which spends their entire life cycle on the dog—from egg to adult—in about a month. They cause intense itching and irritation; as your Maltese scratches, he opens the way to bacterial, viral, or fungal infection. These lice can be discouraged with ordinary flea products. By the way, the human head louse or crab louse can also infect a dog, if it can't find anything better to munch on.

Mites

Ear Mites

Ear mites (*Otodectes cynotis*) infest both the external ear and the ear canal, nibbling away at the loose skin there. Dogs with ear mites shake their heads and dig at their ears. There is usually a nasty discharge, or even a hematoma from self-mutilation. Once your veterinarian confirms that the problem is ear mites, and not a bacterial or fungal infection (which show similar signs), the ear needs to be thoroughly cleaned and then treated with a good commercial ear-mite killer, which are available over the counter.

Mange Mite

The mange mite (*Demodex canis*) is nearly always present on the body of your dog (you have them too—in your eyebrows), but they don't usually cause trouble. Trouble comes in two forms: localized and general. The localized form usually appears on puppies, while the more serious generalized form usually shows up on older dogs. When the disease is present, the mites crowd out the hair follicles, causing them to fall out. The result is hair loss and itchy, swollen, red skin. The localized form often resolves itself without treatment. The generalized form takes intensive therapy, involving dips in the mite and the tick killer amitraz or with oral ivermectin. A complete cure may take up to six months. Generalized demodex is very often a sign that the dog has another problem, such as an autoimmune condition or a serious underlying disease like cancer.

Sarcoptic Mange

Sarcoptic mange, or scabies mite (*Sarcoptes scabei*), is also called "itch mite," and with good reason. The mite burrows into the skin and lays her eggs, which then hatch into larva and dig even deeper into the skin. The results are lesions on many parts of the body, and secondary infections are also common. Both humans and dogs can get sarcoptic mange. People can get a temporary case from their pets, although these mites do not actually reproduce on us. Puppies and young children are more likely to be affected than adults of either species. Affected dogs have a yellowish crust on their skin and matted hair, while human beings get itchy red bumps and a rash. The ears, particularly along the margins, the lateral parts of the elbows, and the ventral parts of the abdomen and thorax are most likely to be affected. This mange is treated with special shampoos, pills, or injections. A good insecticide needs to be applied to the entire area where the dog lives to prevent re-infection.

Walking Dandruff

The charming name of this mite (*Cheyletiella yasguri*) is indicative of its not so charming habit of producing crud and some hair loss on your dog. It doesn't cause the severe itchiness of the other mites and isn't very dangerous. Your veterinarian can treat it easily with amitraz.

Mosquitoes

Mosquitoes carry heartworm disease, and a host of other conditions. If your dog is protected by heartworm preventative, you're

Don't Dip

In the past, people attempted to kill mites by using various dips. I don't recommend this, since certain dips (like organophosphates) can be problematic to dogs. Most mites live too deep in the skin to be affected by dips, and some dips can be toxic to your Maltese. On the other hand, the preferred treatment for demodex is a dip, so always talk to your vet.

a big step ahead. However, in mosquito-infested areas, it wouldn't hurt to use a dog-mosquito repellent too. Although some people claim DEET is safe for dogs, I have my doubts, since dogs tend to lick whatever you spray on their skin. Citronella, a natural repellent, is a safer choice.

Ticks

Ticks are bigger, nastier, and more dangerous than fleas. They carry Lyme disease, Rocky Mountain spotted fever, ehrlichiosis, haemobartonellosis, babesiosis, hepatozoonosis, and a host of other diseases. They don't annoy a dog on the surface as much as fleas do, they don't scamper around, and they don't leave feces everywhere—and that's part of the reason why they're easy to overlook.

Ticks tend to hang out around the head where it's difficult for dogs to reach them. You may also find them between the shoulder blades. Never touch a tick with your bare hands, however. The organism responsible for many tick-borne diseases can sneak in through microscopic cuts in the flesh.

If you find a tick on your Maltese, remove it with tweezers immediately and throw the tick in the toilet. Don't try to burn the tick (too dangerous) or smother it with petroleum jelly (takes too long). Wash your hands immediately afterward, since ticks can give you the same diseases they can give your dog. You can

Check your Maltese for ticks after he's been outside.

protect your dog from tick bites with several excellent products—
talk to your vet about what he or she might recommend.

INTERNAL PARASITES

Internal parasites are usually worms like roundworm,
hookworm, whipworm, and heartworm.

Giardia

Giardia is a common protozoan parasite that can infect any
mammal—including humans. (In fact, it is possible for dog
owners to contract it from their pets.)
Giardia has two life stages: the cyst and
the trophozoite. Dogs can become
infected if they drink cyst-contaminated
water, lick cyst-contaminated feces, or
devour cyst-infected prey. When the
giardia enters the dog's gastrointestinal
systems, they open into the trophozoite
stage, which rapidly reproduce.

To protect your Maltese, keep your
yard picked up, and prevent your dog
from drinking contaminated water
sources. This is tougher than it sounds—
even pristine mountain streams and tap
water can contain the organism.

Lyme Disease Prevention

While there's no really good Lyme prevention for humans,
there is for dogs: amitraz. Amitraz has been used topically
for many years to kill mange mites, but an amitraz collar is
equally effective against the deer tick *Ixodes scapularis*—the
tick that carries the organism responsible for Lyme disease.
Amitraz both repels ticks and paralyzes the mouthparts of
those who manage to climb aboard and try to bite. It also
kills many other species of ticks. Since this treatment is not
without risks, ask your vet. Also, a vaccine against Lyme
disease is available for your dog if ticks are a problem in
your area.

The main symptoms of giardiasis are vomiting and diarrhea in
dogs. Humans report cramping and nausea also, but these
symptoms are difficult to detect in your Maltese. If the condition is
not treated, infected animals can suffer weight loss and continued
periods of vomiting and diarrhea. Several drugs are available to
treat giardiasis, and there is also a vaccine available. Talk over
your options with your veterinarian.

Heartworm

Heartworms are hideous creatures related to roundworms that
live in the right side of the heart and obstruct the heart's large
blood vessels. Badly infected dogs can have hundreds of these
worms in their hearts, and they can live there for years. They lay
very tiny larvae called microfilariae that can live up to three years
in the bloodstream, where they can be sucked up by mosquitoes.

Nearly all puppies are born with roundworms, an easily treatable internal parasite.

During the next two to three weeks in the mosquito, the larvae develop into the infective stage. Then they migrate to the mosquito's mouth and enter a new host.

It takes six to seven months between the time when an animal was bitten until the adult heartworms develop. Signs of infection include coughing, fluid accumulation, decreased appetite, and heart failure. The disease, left untreated, is nearly always fatal. The treatment is risky, long, and difficult, but better than dying from heartworm.

The best cure is prevention. Your vet can prescribe a once-a-month tablet that will keep your Maltese free of heartworms. Any dog can get heartworm—from even one mosquito bite—so take the safe path and keep your dog on medication. Your monthly heartworm pills will kill immature heartworms, but can't be used to kill adult worms. Heartworm medication also prevents your dog from acquiring hookworms, roundworms, and whipworms. Everyone (except the worms) is a winner.

Hookworm

Hookworms can't be seen by the naked eye, but these tiny little devils are all the nastier for that reason. They can penetrate the skin and cause diarrhea and anemia. Hookworms are found mostly in warmer climates; the eggs are passed in the host's feces and develop to the first larval stage if the temperature and humidity are high enough. Clinical signs of hookworm include:

- Intestinal blood loss causing anemia
- Bloody diarrhea
- Weight loss
- Poor hair coat

Puppies are most at risk, since they are less able to handle depleted iron reserves. Humans can also get hookworm. Your vet can diagnose hookworms by fecal flotation. Many antihelmintics are effective against hookworms; treatment usually entails two treatments two weeks apart plus an aggressive preventive program.

Heartworm Fact

There have been cases of heartworm infection in people. Instead of migrating to the heart, the larvae migrate to the lungs.

Roundworm

Roundworms or ascarids are the most common of all internal parasites. They are usually harmless in adult dogs, but can be dangerous when they are passed to puppies through their mothers. (Puppies can still contract them even if the mother has been de-wormed.) Nearly all puppies are born with roundworms, and severely affected puppies can die from them. Infected puppies typically have a rough coat, bad breath, diarrhea, vomiting, and a potbelly. Puppies as young as two weeks can start deworming treatment, which is continued every couple of weeks until the eggs are no longer found in the stool sample.

Tapeworm

Dogs can acquire tapeworms from eating infected fleas (or more rarely, lice). A tapeworm infestation doesn't have many symptoms, and you probably wouldn't even know your pet is affected unless you notice the segments of the worms in his feces. They look like grains of white or pinkish rice. Your vet can prescribe a special de-wormer to rid your Maltese of them.

Whipworm

A severe whipworm infestation can kill your dog. They live in the cecum, the first section of the dog's large intestine, as well as in the large intestine itself. Unfortunately, infestations are often hard to diagnose since the whipworms shed comparatively few eggs. The eggs can live in the ground for years, so it's important to keep your yard picked up every day. A dog may acquire whipworms by accidentally ingesting the infective eggs in contaminated soil. Sometimes your Maltese may show no signs of infection, or you may see:

- Intermittent bouts of diarrhea
- Weight loss
- Anemia
- Dehydration

These things are always more dangerous in small dogs like the Maltese, which have fewer reserves to fight them. Several antihelmintic products are available to whipworms; some of them are also effective against other common dog worms.

FUNGUS

Ringworm

Despite its name, ringworm is a fungus, and a highly contagious one at that. Dogs can pick it up from an infected dog, or even from the ground. It is more common in puppies than in adult dogs. Classical signs include circular, bald patches. In lesion areas, the hair is broken at the base, creating a shaved appearance. Pale skin scales usually occupy the center of the lesion and have a "powdery" appearance, while the edges form a reddened ring. There may be rapid hair loss at the site.

People, especially children, can get ringworm from dogs, so if your Maltese has it, get it treated immediately. Treatment includes disinfecting the environment with bleach, vacuuming, and steam cleaning. Treatment for your Maltese includes oral medications (usually griseofulvin and itraconazole), which must continue for a couple of months to be safe. Or your vet might prefer to use topical treatments or twice-weekly lime sulfur dips. Although ringworm will probably go away (in about four months) on its own, it's much better to treat it right away so that the whole family doesn't come down with it.

Heartworm Tip

Besides the normal round of vaccinations, it's important to keep your Maltese on year-round heartworm preventative, especially if you live in the southern part of the US.

POSSIBLE HEALTH ISSUES FOR MALTESE

All mortal beings fall ill, and while the Maltese is generally a healthy dog, he can, like the rest of the world, get sick. Some diseases common to the Maltese are equally common in other breeds or among dogs in general. Other conditions are more common in Maltese than in the rest of the dog world, and there are still other diseases common in some other breeds that are rare in the Maltese. So don't panic. The list that follows includes a large number of disease conditions, but your Maltese won't get most of them. He may well not get any of them. But there are no guarantees, so preparedness and information are to your advantage.

Addison's Disease (Hypoadrenocorticism)

This is a condition in which parts of the cortisone-producing adrenal glands are only minimally functional. No one knows why it happens, although it is suggested that in most cases the dog's own immune system attacks the adrenal glands. The disease most commonly affects young to middle-aged females. Dogs with Addison's are not able to use glucose correctly or balance levels of sodium and potassium. Signs of Addison's disease include appetite loss, vomiting, diarrhea, and weakness. Since these are also signs of many other diseases, it may take several "tries" to get the right diagnosis. If left untreated, an Addison's dog can go into a crisis which may include kidney failure and low body temperature. At that point, emergency intervention, which would include IV fluids and corticosteroids, is needed to save the dog's life.

Maltese are generally a healthy breed.

With proper medication and careful monitoring by your vet, however, an Addison's dog can live a normal life. However, it is not curable. Today the drug of choice for treating Addison's is Percortin, administered every three or four weeks along with cortisone supplementation like prednisone. Levels may have to be adjusted depending on what kind of stress your dog may be under. Dogs undergoing surgery or exposed to cold weather, for instance, may need more. These are matters you should discuss with your vet.

Allergies

Like human beings, dogs can become allergic to things in their environment. Dogs get several kinds of allergies: inhalant allergies, contact allergies, and food allergies. Dogs tend to respond to allergies by developing skin problems, hair loss, and intense itching, rather than by sneezing.

Omega-3 Fatty Acids

A recent study by veterinary researchers at Colorado State University showed that dogs who were supplemented with omega-3 fatty acids received relief from allergy-related itching.

Contact and Inhalant Allergies

About 15 percent of all dogs today are afflicted with chronic allergic reactions to inhaled particles—anything from maple trees to dust mites. Inhalant allergies tend to be inherited, although no one knows exactly how. We do know that if one or both parents suffer from inhalant allergies, the chances are increased that the puppies will also. The most common culprit is the common household dust mite. Other allergens include trees like elm, maple, and walnut, weeds like lamb's quarters, Russian thistle, ragweed, cocklebur, and English plantain, and various species of grasses. Some dogs are even allergic to human dander!

Grass, plants, bedding, flea collars, floor cleaners, plastic water bowls, and other organic materials are usually the culprits in contact allergies. Unlike inhalant allergies, contact allergies are usually not inherited. Affected dogs can develop lesions, and spend a lot of time chewing their paws. They may show signs of inflammation and itchiness on the rear end, abdomen, and chest where they make contact with the organic material or bedding to which they are allergic. The most effective treatment involves removing the allergen from the dog's environment or submitting the dog to a series of hyposensitization shots. This is effective about 60 percent of the time. Another approach is the use of antihistamines or alternate-day glucocorticoid therapy.

Flea Allergy Dermatitis (FAD)

Many dogs are allergic to flea saliva; it appears that some families of dogs are more susceptible than others. Even one chance bite can produce a reaction. It's not the flea itself to which dogs are allergic, but an anti-coagulant present in the flea's saliva. Dogs show a reaction within a few minutes of being bitten; a second reaction occurs three to four hours later. Crusty scabs may appear towards the rear of the dog. Keep your Maltese flea-free by using the many effective preventative products now on the market.

Food Allergies

Although food allergies are less common than contact or inhalant allergies (5 to 10 percent), many dogs develop allergies to corn, soy, wheat, and certain meat and meat products like beef, pork, chicken, or eggs. All these foods are high in protein. The reason that proteins are so often involved in allergies is that they are very large molecules, each component of which can combine with an antibody or immune system T-cell receptor to produce an allergic reaction.

Food allergies usually show up within 4 to 24 hours of eating the allergenic food, at least in the early stages. Later on, the dog may show symptoms constantly. As in other types of allergies, skin problems (especially around the face or armpits) are the most common signs, but some dogs also vomit, and have diarrhea or gas.

If your Maltese has a year-round itch that doesn't seem affected by weather, you might suspect a food allergy. The only way to test a food allergy is by elimination of suspect foods. He should be placed on a strict elimination diet, which forbids even treats. (Rawhide and dog biscuits often contains dyes to which your pet may be allergic.) The new diet must also contain a protein to which the dog has not previously been exposed (like venison, fish, or rabbit). Further, the dog must stay on that diet for at least 6 weeks. Gradually, suspect foods are added back one at a time. However, the precise substance to which your dog is allergic can be hard to pin down. If you suspect your dog has a food allergy, several manufacturers produce hypo-allergenic diets.

Allergies can cause more than itching, however. In response to the allergen, your Maltese's constant licking and scratching can traumatize the skin, which leaves it open to infection (pyoderma).

Some dogs can develop allergies to foods like corn, soy, and wheat.

Pyoderma can cause *more* itching and pain and inflammation. Ear infections and abscesses beneath the skin may also become part of the pyoderma problem.

Luckily, food allergies do not seem to be inherited. Some Maltese breeders believe a good way to help prevent your Maltese from becoming food allergic is to provide him a varied diet from puppyhood. Don't be afraid to switch foods; it's good for him and challenges his immune system in a positive way.

Arthritis

Arthritis is an inflammation of the joint that typically involves

Dealing With Allergic Reactions

To help protect your dog, take these important steps:

Prevention: Get your dog on flea medication immediately. Probably the most common canine allergy is to fleas, but with the wonderful flea control medicines now on the market, fleas never have to be a problem with your dog again.

Bathing: Use a shampoo appropriate to your dog's needs. Some shampoos are moisturizers; others assist in keeping the skin dry. Some contain soothing aloe, oatmeal, or other natural products. Some are more strongly medicated. Some can be bought by prescription only.

Supplements: Some dog itching is due to poor skin conditioning. If necessary, use a supplement containing omega-3 fatty acid supplements. Most dog foods, especially grocery store brands, are lacking in these vital aids to your Maltese's coat. (Talk to your vet about supplementns, since omega-3 must be given in proper ratio with omega-6, otherwise it can't be absorbed and utilized.)

Antihistamine: Benadryl works well for many dogs, but make sure you get plain Benadryl—not Benadryl with other additives, which can be dangerous to dogs. The usual dose is 1 to 3 milligrams for every pound of dog. Many creams or ointments are also available to help reduce itching. None of these products cure the actual allergies, but they do alleviate the symptoms. This is a critical factor; when dogs don't itch, they don't scratch, and it's the scratching that can produce inflammation and hence infection.

Antibiotics: Your vet may prescribe antibiotics in cases where pyoderma has set in. Many commonly used antibiotics won't work with pyoderma, and your vet may need to take a culture. The course of treatment may be long (over a month).

Cortisone treatment: May be used as a last resort for short term use only. I would avoid this unless your Maltese is suffering acutely and no other treatment is beneficial. Some types of cortisone injections can be especially dangerous.

Quit smoking: Smoke allergies are common, and if your Maltese suffers any other kind of allergy, your smoking will only make it worse. Quit now.

degradation of cartilage surrounding the bone, causing joint pain, stiffness, and reduced range of motion. All dogs, like all people, are vulnerable to this condition as they age, but trauma can also produce it. Once arthritis starts, it will gradually worsen. While there is no cure for arthritis, it can be treated and managed. Your dog's diet, weight, and level of activity can all be customized to reduce the pain and inconvenience of the disease. Non-steroidal anti-inflammatory drugs (NSAIDS), glucosamine-chondroitin supplements, and moderate exercise can help reduce the pain. Talk to your vet about the best pain management for your dog.

Food Allergy Fact

Your dog could be allergic to any dietary ingredient, including dye in medicine or flavoring in treats. Feed your dog a diet that does not include artificial flavors, dyes, or preservatives.

Cancer

Cancer is the leading disease-related cause of death in pet dogs, killing more than 4,000 animals every year. Cancer isn't really one disease: it's a general term for more than 200 different types of malignancies that can affect any part of the body. All cancers, however, work basically the same way: they result from too rapid cell growth; the cells are all "undifferentiated," meaning that they can no longer be recognized as a liver cell, or skin cell, or whatever kind of the cell they were supposed to be. Cancer cells also have apparently developed something like an "immortality gene," and so unlike normal cells that are born and die, cancer cells just go on indefinitely.

While we're still unsure about all the factors that go into making cancer, scientists believe that hormones may be partly to blame, especially in cancers that affect the reproductive system and thyroid. Hormones may stimulate an abnormal cell to divide and develop into a tumor.

For many types of cancer, a higher-fat, low carbohydrate diet is a must. Cancer cells steal energy from carbohydrates; fight back by feeding your dog fats, which provide more energy but are difficult for cancer cells to access.

New treatments for cancer are on the horizon. One promising new route, still experimental, is brachytherapy. In this procedure, doctors introduce radiation-emitting beads directly into the tumor site using a hollow tube. This operation lets the doctor target the cancer very directly without affecting other tissues.

Another new treatment involves the use of angiogenesis inhibitors, a special kind of chemotherapy that "starves" tumors by killing their blood supply. The veterinarian may use a cocktail

Common Signs of Cancer

According to the Veterinary Cancer Society, here are common signs of cancer in small animals (and notice how similar these signs are to cancer in human beings):

- Abnormal swellings that persist or continue to grow
- Sores that don't heal
- Weight loss
- Loss of appetite
- Bleeding or discharge from any body opening
- Offensive odor
- Difficulty eating or swallowing
- Hesitation to exercise or loss of stamina
- Persistent lameness or stiffness
- Difficulty breathing, urinating, or defecating

For more information, go to www.vetcancersociety.org/owners.htm

of drugs for this purpose, including drugs originally prescribed for people. One such cocktail included Celebrex (arthritis medication for humans), the breast cancer drug tamoxifen, and the antibiotic doxycycline used to fight acne in people and Lyme disease in dogs.

It's important to know that no one cancer treatment is right for every dog. Age and even personality type may dictate the best kind of treatment. Some cancers are rather readily cured. Costs can also vary widely, ranging from little more than average surgery or medication costs to several thousand dollars.

Lumps and Bumps

A lump on your dog could be as simple as a cyst or scar tissue or something very serious like a malignant tumor. There is no way to tell by looking at it. If your Malt has a suspicious lump, especially one that is fast growing or seems attached to the bone, call your vet—only he or she can tell for sure. Your vet may decide to biopsy it or may decide to remove it right away. Until the lump is diagnosed, it's not possible to properly treat it. It is better to be overly cautious than to ignore the problem. Don't let fear keep you from the vet—many lumps, even cancerous ones, are treatable if caught early.

Important questions to be addressed include:

- Is the lump painful, bleeding, itchy or tender?
- Does it seem attached to the bone?
- Is there only one lump or multiple similar lumps?
- Is it growing in size?
- Is it soft or hard?
- How long has it been there and how has it changed?
- How old is your Maltese?
- Where is the lump?
- Is the dog exhibiting other "sick signs" such as vomiting?

Canine Influenza Virus: The New Dog Flu

A new canine flu virus has appeared, first among racing Greyhounds, and now among pets generally. No one knows where it came from, but experts think the original was another kind of horse influenza that made a trans-species jump (viruses are very smart that way). The new virus goes by several names, including canine influenza virus, Greyhound disease, and race flu.

This disease is not kennel cough, although is bears a superficial resemblance to it. The flu is caused by a virus that produces coughing, high fevers, nasal discharge and, horribly, a fatal pneumonia in some animals. It is highly contagious. While most dogs will only have mild coughing, puppies and older dogs are at greater risk. Dogs housed in close quarters at kennels are most likely to be infected. While the virus is airborne, it can also spread on clothing or other objects that have been in contact with the dog. The incubation period is believed to be 2 to 5 days. Signs include irritated eyes, runny nose, sneezing, coughing, high fever (there is no fever with kennel cough), and depression. If your dog shows signs of any of these, see your vet. While there is no cure, supportive treatment can be helpful.

Cushing's Disease

Cushing's disease occurs when the body produces too much cortisol, a steroid hormone produced by the adrenal glands which is critical for normal body function. In some older dogs, usually because of a tumor in the pituitary gland or even on the adrenal gland itself, excess cortisol is produced. Too much cortisol can reduce the ability of the kidneys to reabsorb water, so the dog tends to urinate more frequently and drink more water. The excess cortisol also seems to affect the appetite center of the brain and to make some dogs extremely hungry all the time.

A new canine flu has appeared that may affect your Maltese if he spends time in boarding kennels.

When there's too much cortisol over a long period of time, the result is muscle wasting, fat redistribution, and an enlarged liver. Many Cushing's dogs have a distinctive "pot-bellied" appearance. They also may lose hair symmetrically in the trunk area and have skin infections. (Too much cortisol suppresses the immune function.)

There are several available treatments for Cushing's. If the tumor is on the adrenal gland, it may be possible to remove it surgically. In other cases, medications are available that can decrease, at least temporarily, the amount of cortisol produced. With good medical treatment, your dog's lifespan may be increased by 18 months, which can be a long time for a dog.

Diabetes

The body needs glucose (sugar)—it is the main energy supplier of the cells. However, it's the remarkable hormone we know as insulin, which is produced in the pancreas, that allows the body cells to use that glucose. A diabetic dog is one who simply doesn't have enough insulin. The cells in the body think there's no glucose to feed them, even though the dog might have just eaten a pound of sugar. In fact, what often happens is that when the cells think they're starving, actually a surplus of unused glucose has been building up in the bloodstream the whole time. So the dog is in the curious state of having at once too much and too little glucose—not a good state of affairs. There is so much glucose in the blood that the kidney can't manage it all and it spills over into the urine. The glucose takes a lot of water with it, and the dog experiences tremendous thirst. And of course, he is very hungry, thinking he's starved all the time. These are main signs of diabetes:

- Excessive thirst
- Excessive hunger
- Excessive urination
- Weight loss

Later on, the dog may develop cataracts, because the glucose has entered the lens of the eye. The diabetic dog is also extremely prone to urinary tract infections, because all the sugar in there is a perfect breeding ground for bacteria.

Once your vet determines your Malt has diabetes, he will probably prescribe insulin. Follow your veterinarian's instructions—please don't alter the prescribed dose. You will probably need to buy a new bottle of insulin every six to eight weeks, no matter how much of it you will actually use. Your vet will teach you how to give the injection.

Diabetic dogs benefit from two equal-sized meals about 12 hours apart. Your vet may recommend a high fiber diet, if your Maltese can tolerate it. Under no circumstances, though, should you take a tough love approach and try to starve your pet into accepting a high fiber diet. The results could be disastrous. It's essential that your diabetic Maltese get regular meals.

Your vet will work with you and show you how to use a dipstick to monitor the glucose in your dog's urine every morning. If your Malt suddenly starts acting drunk, it may mean the blood sugar has dropped too low. If that happens, give him a tablespoon or so of Karo syrup. If you don't see immediate improvement, get him to the vet—it's an emergency.

Ear Problems

Deafness

Some Maltese suffer from an inherited deafness, for which there is no cure. The best prevention is to make sure the puppy is not deaf when you choose him (see Chapter 3).

Most older dogs experience some loss of hearing, and as we mentioned earlier, some Maltese are congenitally deaf. However, the process is usually so slow that you may not realize it has happened, especially if you own one of those dogs who never paid any attention to you even when he could hear you. You can usually get their attention by stamping on the floor, turning lights on or off, or using a laser pointer.

It is critically important to keep these dogs on a leash at all times when not in your house or in the yard under your supervision. Attach a loud bell to his collar. If he gets away, he won't be able to hear you, but you may be able to hear

Diabetes Tip

If your female Maltese is intact, and she is diagnosed with diabetes, get her spayed immediately. Progesterone interferes with insulin.

Deaf dogs can be taught to respond to hand signals.

his bell ringing!

When waking up a deaf dog, always touch him very gently on the shoulder (that's the safest place). If you have one of those dogs who "comes up swinging" use a long pole to wake him. No point in getting bitten accidentally. You can gradually desensitize your dog to this startle reflex to some degree by touching him frequently and always giving a treat when you do so.

Dogs who have gone completely deaf can learn to respond to hand signals. You can even buy vibrating (*not electric shock*) collars to help train your dog, although most dogs do just fine without them. For more information visit the Deaf Dog Education Fund at: www.deafdogs.org.

If your dog is amenable he can actually relearn commands in a simplified version of American Sign language. You can make up your own signals, too, of course. The common sign for "Good!" is smiling and clapping your hands together. Most dogs learn this one really fast, especially if there is a treat involved.

Infections

Dogs with drop ears like the Maltese are more prone to all kinds of ear trouble than are erect-eared dogs. One of the most common is otitis externa or inflammation of the ear canal. This condition can be caused by all kind of things, including parasites (such as ear mites and ticks), microorganisms, foreign bodies, tumors, and underlying skin disease. (Remember that the ears are just an extension of the skin.)

Yeast infections of the ear are extremely common—the most usual culprit is Malassezia pachydermatitis. Signs include head

Good to Know

Recurring ear infections may indicate an allergic reaction.

shaking and scratching, as well as a characteristic "yeasty" odor. Bacteria such as Staphylococci, Streptococci, E. coli, and Pseudomonas may also show up, often at the same time as the yeast. A vet can swab the ear and examine the exudates under a microscope to determine the precise cause of the problem. Treatment usually consists of flushing and drying the ear, as well as other medication as needed. If your Maltese suffers from recurrent ear infections, suspect allergies or even hypothyroidism (especially if other signs are present).

Keeping your dog's ears well cared for, and plucking the ear canal hair will often result in fewer or no infections. Clean the ears weekly with a good commercial ear cleaner, and always after bathing. You certainly don't want your Maltese to get "swimmer's ear!"

Is it Ear Mites?

Ear mites are much more common in cats than they are in dogs. Don't assume they are responsible for your dog's ear condition unless confirmed by a vet. If your dog does have them, possibly other animals in the house do as well.

Eye Problems

Aberrant Cilia and Distichiasis

These congenital conditions refer to eyelashes (cilia) growing in weird directions, often rubbing against the cornea and leading to a corneal ulcer. Many people consider distichiasis a particular form of aberrant cilia in which there are two sets of eyelashes, with the extra hair rubbing against the cornea or eyelids. The condition is treated surgically under general anesthesia, with a procedure called cryoepilation.

Conjunctivitis

Conjunctivitis is an inflammatory problem of the mucous membranes of the eye. It is the most common eye disease in dogs. It is usually caused by a virus or bacteria, although parasites, dust, fungi, or allergies may also cause it. If the white portion of the eyeball is also inflamed, it may be called "pink eye." Signs include reddened mucous membranes and a clear or colored discharge. Clear, mucoid discharges are usually associated with allergies or irritants. A sticky yellow or green discharge is a sign of infection. The eyelids may even stick together when held shut. The eyes are usually itchy, and your Maltese may paw at them or rub is face along the furniture or on the floor. Eye drops or ointments are usually the drugs of choice. In severe cases, oral antibiotics are used in addition to the topical therapy.

Some Maltese are prone to eye problems—make sure you check his eyes regularly.

Glaucoma

Glaucoma is the most common cause of blindness in dogs, and Maltese are prone to it. This is a painful condition where pressure inside the eyeball increases to dangerous levels because small drains within the eyeball are narrowed or blocked. The result is usually permanent damage to the retina causing severe pain and blindness. Often the cause is heritable, but the disease can also result from injury, tumors, or infections. Your dog's eyes should be checked very carefully after the age of eight.

While both people and dogs can get glaucoma, there's an important difference. With people the disease progresses slowly and often painlessly. With dogs, it often has a fast onset, is excruciatingly painful, and is a veterinary emergency. Unfortunately, dogs are so stoic that you may not even know your dog has the problem unless you are very alert for its signs: squinting, redness, and cloudiness.

Your vet will measure the eye pressure with a tonometer, and if necessary begin emergency treatment. In cases where the pressure has been caused by some physical plugging of the "drain" in the eye, like a tumor, chronic uveitis, or lens luxation, sight may be restored. However, in hereditary glaucoma, sight will usually eventually be lost in both eyes. However, the disease still needs to be treated, sometimes requiring the removal of the blind eye, to stop the pain.

Keratoconjunctivitis Sicca (KCS)

KCS occurs when there is insufficient moisture in the eye. Dogs with this condition usually have a thick mucous discharge. Eventually an ulcer may develop. Treatment involves tear stimulants, artificial tears, and anti-inflammatory medication.

Progressive Retinal Atrophy

This is a hereditary disease that produces a gradually progressing night blindness, which ultimately leads to total blindness. Early signs include dilated pupils or brighter "eyeshine" at night. The condition is irreversible, but painless. No effective medical treatment is known.

If Your Maltese Goes Blind

Partial, if not total, loss of sight is common in older dogs. It can be caused by glaucoma, corneal problems, cancer, trauma, retinal diseases or cataracts. Blind dogs require some extra care, but can enjoy long and full lives. It is not the tragedy for them that it is for humans, and in point of fact, blindness seems to bother the dog owners more than it does the dog, who lives in a universe of rich smells and vibrant sounds.

If you are patient with your blind dog, conservative about moving furniture around, and willing to make a few adjustments to his new lifestyle, there's no reason why he can't go on happily for many years more.

Don't baby your blind dog. He still enjoys walks and being outside in your company. Of course, don't leave him alone outside, or indoors in a strange place or with new furniture. Use a crate when he's by himself until he knows the house very well. Block his access to stairs. Talk to him, give him squeaky toys, and try in every way to enrich his world of sound and smell.

Give him time and he will learn to navigate his way around. In fact, if the blindness has been coming on gradually, he may have already learned to do this so well that it comes as a surprise to discover he's blind! Be consistent about his feeding and sleeping areas and speak to him before touching him. Make sure you don't clip off his whiskers, which he can use as little guides around the rooms. I know one dog once who carried a stuffed toy in his mouth and used it as a "bumper." In fact, you can purchase a harness-like device that acts much in the same way, although most dogs seem preternaturally able to guide themselves.

Of course you can help by being super conscious of open doors, fireplaces, hot tubs, and sharp objects located at doggy eye-level. Put a note on his collar that states he is blind, in the awful event he becomes lost. For support and more information, visit the Owners of Blind Dogs Website at www.blinddogs.com.

Heart Disease

Heart disease comes in two basic varieties: congenital and acquired. The latter type occurs in many older dogs of all breeds.

Veterinary Ophthalmologists

For a list of qualified veterinary ophthalmologists by state, please visit www.malteseonly.com /eyedocs.html

Good breeding is the best way to prevent many diseases.

In some cases, the problem is with the valves of the heart, which for one reason or another fail to close properly and cause an abnormal blood flow. In other cases, the walls of the heart gradually become thin and weak. Both conditions result in heart failure, a condition affecting millions of dogs. In heart failure, the heart has to work harder and to pump the required amount of blood. It becomes enlarged, and the dog may cough and have difficulty breathing. While there is no cure for heart failure, there are several available treatments, which are most successful if begun early.

Hypoglycemia

Hypoglycemia means there is a sudden drop of glucose in the blood, and it is frequently seen in the Maltese. This is primarily a disease of puppies, with Maltese vulnerable between the ages of five to nine weeks, and then again at about six months of age. Signs include weakness, wobbly legs, pale gums, and drooling. It may be preventable by adding a bit of extra glucose in the form or honey to your puppy's meal. He will probably outgrow it when he reaches adulthood.

Hypothyroidism

Hypothyroidism is the most common hormone imbalance in

dogs. Dogs with this condition have inadequate production of the thyroid hormones. When the thyroid gland malfunctions, every cell in the body is affected. The hair becomes brittle, sparse, and coarse, and is easily pulled out. The dog may be lethargic and his eyelids will droop. The average age for a dog to develop a low thyroid condition is between the ages of 3 and 5; most cases are inherited. A blood test (for T4, the main thyroid hormone, and canine TSH, the thyroid stimulating hormone from the pituitary gland) can detect the disease, and your vet will put your dog on an inexpensive thyroid supplement (L-thyroxine) as a lifelong treatment.

Kidney and Urinary Problems

Chronic Renal Failure

This is the most common kidney problem in dogs. It can be congenital, genetic, acquired, or of unknown cause. The kidneys not only control water in the body but also help keep blood pressure in check, maintain electrolyte balance, and eliminate water soluble products like urea. Early signs of renal failure include weight loss, irritability, poor coat condition, dehydration, and lethargy. Ulcers may form in the mouth. Your Maltese may drink and urinate more than usual, sometimes urinating in inappropriate places.

If your vet suspects chronic renal failure, he or she may suggest blood work, urinalysis, or radiographs. Although the condition worsens over time, good care can help. This may include IV fluid therapy, potassium supplementation, and a special low-protein, low-phosphate diet, now available commercially.

Glomerular Disease

The glomerulus is the microscopic kidney area that removes small metabolic toxins from the blood, separating urine from the blood. In glomerulonephritis, chronic inflammation leads to holes in the filtration system, allowing large molecules (that the body needs to keep) to enter the urine. It can be caused by neglected dental disease, cancer, heartworm infection, ehrlichia, Lyme disease, immune mediated disease, endocarditis, pancreatitis, and other conditions. Signs include weight loss, stomach upset, and classical renal failure. Severe cases may result in "Nephrotic Syndrome." This syndrome includes significant protein loss in urine, low serum albumin, edema, and elevated blood cholesterol level. Treatment depends upon determining the cause. Your vet can discuss your options with you.

Urinary Tract Infections and Bladder Stones

A number of factors can cause urinary infections in dogs— everything from bacteria overgrowth to bladder stones. Bladder stones form from a single irritating particle called a nidus (they are sort of like pearls, in a way). This nidus collects a progressively larger coating of minerals which can, over time, become irritating to the lining of the bladder. If a bladder stone gets lodged in the urethra, it becomes difficult for the animal to urinate. If the vet suspects bladder stones, he or she will take an x-ray and perhaps do an ultrasound examination. Bladder stones come in several varieties, and it's important to determine the type of stone before treatment is begun. Some kinds can be dissolved by medication, while others, like ones made of calcium oxalate, cannot. These stones must be removed surgically.

There are some genetic conditions that affect certain lines of Maltese.

Medial Patellar Luxation

This condition, which is a dislocation of the kneecap, is a common problem in all small breeds like the Maltese. It is mostly hereditary in nature, but can also be influenced by the environment. Medial patellar luxation is generally classified by grade, from 1 to 4.

- Grade 1 luxations may not cause lameness, but can be detected during the physical exam because the kneecap is fairly easy to push out of its groove.
- Grade 2 luxations are slightly more severe and cause the dog to occasionally carry one hind leg in a skipping motion.
- Grade 3 luxations cause obvious lameness; the dog usually carries the leg up without letting it touch the ground.
- Grade 4 luxations usually involve visible deformity of the leg and severe lameness.

Dogs with only Grade 1 are often not treated, unless the dog is very young. Young dogs with Grade 2 or above patellar luxations probably should have corrective surgery; adults with Grade 3 or above luxations should have corrective surgery. There are several possible surgical procedures for this disorder and the surgery should be done by a specialist and as soon as possible. However, I should mention that a lot of dogs who are not treated surgically for this condition do pretty well, even though they are in some pain.

Liver Shunt

A portosystemic shunt is a genetic condition affecting some lines of Maltese. Portosystemic shunts are abnormal vascular connections between the hepatic portal vein (which connects the gastrointestinal tract with the liver) and the systemic circulation. Such a condition seriously degrades the ability of the liver to function properly and can be fatal.
Signs include:

- failure to grow
- depression or lethargy
- temporary blindness
- weakness (especially after eating)

Most affected dogs are under one year old, but older dogs can be affected as well. Your vet can diagnose the problem with routine lab work, radiographs, or liver function testing.

The aim of therapy for this disease is to get the liver to work better. Treatment may consist of surgical ligation (a procedure that should be attempted only by a vet with experience in this area). Medical management may include dietary changes such as switching to a restricted but higher-quality protein food. Oral antibiotics may also be prescribed to kill of some of the bacteria that produce ammonia in the intestine, as well as lactulose. This is something that needs to be decided on a case by case basis.

Pancreatitis

Pancreatitis is inflammation of the pancreas. Pancreatitis is a common disease of dogs, and may occur after a dog has eaten a high-fat meal. Signs include loss of appetite, vomiting, abdominal pain, and depression. In severe cases, it can be fatal. Take your Maltese to the vet for treatment.

White Shaker Dog Syndrome

This is a diffuse tremor of the whole body. It gets its name because it usually affects small white dogs, mostly Maltese, but also West Highland White Terriers and occasionally Poodles, Bichon Frise, or even Beagles. Most victims are young adults (6 months to 3 years of age). No one knows the exact cause, although some speculate that there is a generalized neurotransmitter deficiency due to an autoimmune reaction. The tremors get progressively worse for a couple of days, and then remain the same until treatment is started. There may be rapid eye movements, too. Tremors are worse when the animal attempts to do something. (The fancy name for this is an "intention" tremor.) The disease is not painful, so far as we know. Most dogs recover completely with early treatment with corticosteroids, benzodiazepines or both. Your veterinarian will start your dog at a relatively high dose that is gradually decreased over several weeks. Some dogs need to stay on a low dosage on alternate days for life.

WHAT YOU SHOULD KNOW ABOUT LAB TESTS

Here are some common tests to which your Maltese may be subjected, and what they might indicate.

Complete Blood Count (CBC)

The CBC measures the number and types of cells circulating in the bloodstream. Decreased red blood cells produces the condition we know as anemia. Too many red blood cells usually suggest dehydration. A low count of neutrophils (white blood cells) may indicate bone marrow disease or a virus. A high level indicates inflammation or infection.

Packed Cell Volume (PCV)

PCV is the percent of red blood cells compared to the total volume of blood. In normal dogs and cats, 40-50 percent of the blood is made up of blood cells and the rest is fluid.

Chemistry Panel

A chemistry panel measures various substances in the blood, such as:

- **Albumin**: a small protein produced by the liver. Decreased albumin can indicate liver damage, a damaged intestine, or kidney disease. Increased albumin indicates dehydration.
- **Alkaline phosphatase**: high levels indicate liver disease or bone disease. Increased blood cortisol from drugs or Cushing's disease may also cause it.
- **ALT (SGPT) and AST (SGOT)**: liver-produced enzymes that increase if there is liver damage.
- **Amylase and Lipase**: Amylase is an enzyme produced by the pancreas and the intestinal tract; increased levels may indicate pancreatitis or cancer of the pancreas. Lipase is another pancreatic enzyme that breaks down fats. Increased levels may also indicate pancreatitis or cancer
- **Bile acids**: produced by the liver help break down fat. Dogs with abnormal blood flow to the liver may have abnormal levels of bile acids.
- **Bilirubin**: waste product produced by the liver from old red blood cells. It is higher in dogs with certain kinds of liver

What are Glucocorticoids?

Glucocorticoids (prednisone and prednisolone) are commonly prescribed medications, although few people know exactly how they work, or even what they are! Glucocorticoids are hormones that break down stored fat, sugar, and proteins in the body to use in times of stress. They also are anti-inflammatory and immune-suppressive, and this is usually why they are prescribed. The adrenal glands produce them naturally in the body. Your vet may prescribe glucocorticoids for joint pain, itchy skin, cancer (especially for lymphoma), central nervous system disorders, and blood calcium reduction. They can also unmask hidden infections.

The drugs do have side effects however, such as excessive thirst and urination. Higher doses can be irritating to the stomach. In addition, these drugs should not be used at the same time as Rimadyl or other NSAIDs; the combination could cause stomach ulcers or serious problems like kidney or liver failure or fatal anemia. Diabetic and pregnant dogs should not take these medications. The medication may also change liver enzyme and thyroid blood testing.

When prednisone is prescribed for a long period of time, its use needs to be tapered off gradually, not suddenly stopped. Suddenly stopping the medication doesn't give the adrenal glands enough warning to start producing the normal amount of glucocorticoids on their own.

Always ask your vet if you don't understand what a lab test result indicates.

disease, gallbladder disease, or in patients with hemolysis, a condition in which the red blood cells are being destroyed at a faster than normal rate.

- **Blood urea nitrogen (BUN)**: a waste product produced by the liver. A low BUN can be seen with liver disease and an increased BUN is seen in pets with kidney disease or dehydration.
- **Calcium**: high blood calcium is most commonly associated with cancer, although it can also be caused by chronic kidney failure, primary hyperparathyroidism, poisoning, and bone disease. Low blood calcium results from a malfunction of the parathyroid glands, which produce a hormone (PTH) that controls blood calcium levels, or poisoning with antifreeze.
- **Cholesterol**: a lipid which can be increased in dogs with hypothyroidism, Cushing's disease, diabetes and kidney diseases that cause protein to be lost in the urine. However, high cholesterol in dogs does not seem to produce heart and blood vessel disease the way it does in people.
- **Creatinine**: a waste product excreted by the kidneys. High levels indicate kidney disease or dehydration.
- **Creatinine kinase**: an enzyme, which in elevated levels indicates damage to the muscle, including heart muscle.
- **Glucose (blood sugar)**: high levels indicate diabetes mellitus, and mildly increased levels are sometimes present in dogs with Cushing's disease. Low blood sugar is less frequent and may signal pancreatic cancer or overwhelming infection.
- **Phosphorus**: a mineral that is elevated in dogs with chronic kidney disease.
- **Potassium**: higher than normal levels of this mineral indicate acute kidney failure, Addison's disease, or a ruptured or obstructed bladder.
- **Sodium**: high levels of this mineral may indicate dehydration; low blood sodium is most commonly seen with Addison's disease.

Urinalysis

Your vet may also request a urine sample. The concentration, color, clarity, and microscopic examination of the urine sample can provide diagnostic information about several body systems. In some cases you'll be responsible for collecting the urine. The easiest method is the old "free catch" method in which you take the dog for a walk and slip a clean plastic container underneath when he lifts his leg. If you must wait for a period before going to the vet, you can cover the container and keep it in the refrigerator, but don't tell the family. If for some reason you can't manage that, the urine can be collected at the clinic with a urinary catheter.

Your vet will check the sediment in the urine for increased white blood cells (possibly indicating a bladder infection, quite common in females). Diabetic dogs may have increased glucose in the urine. The vet will also measure the specificity gravity of the urine—an abnormal level can mean kidney disease. Bladder stones can give away their presence by leaving silica crystals in the urine; ammonium biurate crystals signal liver problems. Solid lumps of protein cells called casts suggestions a problem with the tubules in the kidney.

ASKING QUESTIONS

As I mentioned, more than likely your Maltese will never be diagnosed with any of these potential diseases. However, if you do end up dealing with a serious problem, or even something very common and treatable, you need to make sure you understand the problem and the treatment. I often get calls from people who say, "My vet says my dog has Carpiothyburoforkoliosis (or whatever). How bad is that? Should he be on a special diet? Is it catching?"

I always ask, "Well, I dunno. What did your vet say?"

"I didn't ask." Or, "he told me but I forgot." Or, "He told me but I didn't understand what he meant."

Don't be afraid to ask your veterinarian questions. Here are some of the most important ones, if your dog has been diagnosed with a serious ailment:

- "What does my dog have, exactly?" Get both the official medical name for the disorder as well as a down-to-earth explanation of what it means.
- "What's the prognosis?" This means you're asking your vet to predict the final outcome of the disease. Is the disease curable? Treatable? If not, will it eventually kill your dog? These are hard questions, but you need to know.

Diagnostic Imaging

Today's vets can take advantage of many high-tech procedures to help see what is going on with your dog.

X-ray: the most familiar imaging tool, the x-rays are projected through the patient onto x-ray sensitive film. They pass through soft tissues easily, but are blocked by bone, so bones will look clear, a cavity dark, and soft tissues gray.

CAT-scan: another tool is the CAT (computerized axial tomography)-scan. Here a very thin beam of x-rays passes through a cross-section of the body in a rotational manner. The beam can be adjusted to show very specific image slices, like the skull one section at a time. A computer can also use the scan to create a three-dimensional image. The CAT-scan is very useful in determining subtle variations in tissue.

MRI (magnetic resonance imaging): uses radio waves and powerful magnetic fields to create images. It creates a vibration in the fluid found in the body which in turn emits a radio signal. A receptor coil produces a cross-sectional image of body water content found in the tissues. Bones are not shown (too little water), but this imaging gives the best views of soft tissues like the liver or brain.

Ultrasound: uses high frequency sound waves to detect problems in the heart, spleen, or liver, as well as the movement of fetuses.

All these diagnostic tools require special training, and many are expensive, cumbersome, and unsuited to an all-purpose veterinary practice, which may have only an x-ray machine.

• "What's the best course of action and how will it help my dog?" Your vet may want to prescribe medication, do surgery, radiation, herbs, or acupuncture, so you need to find out what he wants to do and how it will help.

• "How will this disease and its treatment affect my dog?" You'll want to know if your dog will be listless, lose his appetite, or have problems with housetraining. If the disease is transmittable to your other dogs, you want to know that also.

• "What responsibility will I have in his care?" Your dog's illness may require you to medicate him regularly, or even take him for treatments elsewhere.

• "How much will this cost?" This is a fair and legitimate question. Ask it.

• "Should my pet see a specialist?" Veterinary medicine has almost as many specialists as human medicine does. You're not insulting your general practitioner vet if you ask his recommendation to see an oncologist, ophthalmologist, or whatever specialist your dog may require.

Get everything in writing. Don't leave until you completely understand. If you get home and realize you forgot to ask something, call your vet back. If you are not satisfied with something and can't work it out, see a different vet. There's no profit in wandering about in ignorance or uncertainty.

ALTERNATIVE AND COMPLEMENTARY VETERINARY MEDICINE

While there is no replacement for modern western veterinary care, we can also take advantage of other modalities of care, including Chinese and Western herbal medicine and acupuncture.

Acupuncture

Acupuncture actually began as a practice in China thousands of years ago; however, scientists are still not sure how it works. According to Chinese thought, a system of life energy or Qi (pronounced "chee" and sometimes spelled "chi") circulates through the body along meridians, special pathways through the body. Acupuncture points lie along these meridians and when stimulated with fine needles the acupuncturist can manipulate the energy flows. Acupuncture has been shown to improve hip dysplasia, arthritis, certain gastrointestinal ailments, skin problems, hormone imbalances, and some cancers and diseases of the nervous system. To find a veterinary acupuncturists (and there are more than 1,000 of them) search the site of the International Veterinary Acupuncture Society (IVAS) at www.ivas.org or the American Academy of Veterinary Acupuncturists (www.aava.org).

You might want to take advantage of some alternative modalities of care.

Chiropractic

Another alternative therapy is chiropractic, purpose of which is to get the neuro-muscular-skeletal system aligned by using gentle manipulations. It also helps to keep the joints flexible. Not all veterinarians approve of chiropractic procedures, but many people have had great success with them. Chiropractic can be used effectively for dogs with disc problems, hip dysplasia, and arthritis. You should expect to see improvement after a few treatments. For a list of certified veterinary chiropractors near you, contact the American Veterinary Chiropractic Association (AVCA) at www.animalchiropractic.org or the American Holistic Medical Association at www.ahvma.org. There are currently more than 350 veterinarians and chiropractors certified to treat animals.

Flower Essences

This branch of alternative medicine was developed in England early in the twentieth century by Edward Bach. Today there are approximately 50,000 active practitioners of the art all over the world. The theory behind flower essence therapy is called resonance, and healers caution that they work best when the essence you select matches the core emotional challenges the dog faces (if you can figure out what they are). Flower essences aren't designed for physical ailments, but rather for psychological and emotional problems that can develop into physical distress.

Although there are 38 different combinations of flower essences in Bach's pharmacopeias (and more than 200 other blends developed since), the most well known today is Bach's special blend of five flower essences. It is produced and sold under various names such as Rescue Remedy and Five Flower Formula. This particular decoction is widely marketed for its calming effect on nervous and stressed dogs.

Flower essences are usually administered in a dose of four drops four times a day. Flower essence therapy is best suited for animals with emotionally-based problems, and the essences can be rubbed into the gums or added to some bread and fed to the dog. Flower essence therapy requires frequent application, as its effects seem transient. It is often combined with other kinds of therapy, particularly herbs and essential oils. In my opinion, much like homeopathy (discussed below), flower essence therapy "works" because it doesn't do anything to worsen the condition. Others believe its effects are more positive.

Herbs

Herbalism is of growing interest to dog owners who are looking for alternatives to western medications. There are several approaches to the study of herbs, among them Traditional Chinese Medicine, Western Herbalism, and Ayurvedic Medicine, which originated in India and the Middle East. Although each branch of herbal medicine has a slightly different emphasis, all work by helping the body maintain its own health. This approach is in contradistinction to conventional western medicine, which operates by focusing on the disease process rather than on wellness.

Using herbs as medicine is not necessarily a do-it-yourself approach. Herbalism is a complex science, like conventional medicine, and best results are obtained when you visit a qualified veterinary herbalist. Many such practitioners also have a degree in veterinary medicine. No one should approach herbal medication as a "quick fix." Most herbs act more slowly than do the potent drugs which partly derive from them. Several days may pass before the patient sees improvement. Nor are herbs some kind of "wonder drug" that will magically eliminate all your pet's diseases. They are simply a method of treatment. Not every one will work on every disease, and some diseases have no cures at all, herbal or otherwise. In addition, herbs lack the purity of laboratory tested medications, and the dosages are not so precise.

That doesn't mean, however, that herbs are of no use. They can often alleviate pain and relieve symptoms. Too often people use both herbs and drugs to treat the symptoms, and are then

Herbal Medicines

Here are some of the most popular herbs, and their common usages:

Aloe vera (*Aloe spp.*): promotes healing and can be used as a laxative

Burdock (*Arctium lappa*): helps seborrhea

Cayenne (*Capsicum spp.*): helps circulation

Chamomile (*Matricaria recutita*): helps indigestion and flatulence; aslo for calming

Dandelion (*Taraxacum officale*): diuretic; provides vitamins and minerals

Echinacea or coneflower (*Echinacea spp.*): boosts the immune system

Fennel (*Foeniculum vulgare*): helps indigestion and flatulence

Gingko (*Gingko biloba*): helps urinary tract health and mental stimulation

Licorice (*Glycyrrhiza glabra*): anti-inflammatory

Nettle (*Urtica spp.*): helps conjunctivitis and dermatitis; provides vitamins and minerals

Oregon grape (*Mahonia aquifolium*): anti-inflammatory; antimicrobial

Raspberry leaf (*Rubus idaeus*): helps conjunctivitis; astringent

Red clover (*Trifolium pratense*): helps skin problems, swollen lymph nodes

Sage (*Salvia officinalis*): antimicrobial

Skullcap (*Scutellaria spp.*): helps anxiety, relieves pain

Slippery elm (*Ulmus fulva*): gastrointestinal or urinary infection

Yucca (*Achillea millefolium*): reduces inflammation

disappointed and surprised to find out that the disease itself remains. It's always important to remember that treating a symptom and treating the underlying condition don't necessarily call for the same herbal or drug regimen.

Just as with conventional medications, herbal dosages vary from case to case. Luckily, however, herbs are much more "forgiving" in this regard than are western-style drugs. If you are using herbs on your Maltese, you should work out the dosages with your animal herbalist. Most herbalists also recommend that your dog take a break from herbal medication two days a week. Overdoses of herbal medications can be toxic, just as with conventional medications. Signs of overdose include vomiting, diarrhea, and itching. Simply because something is herbal, doesn't mean that it cannot be dangerous in large doses. Comfrey, for example, contains a fair amount of pyrrolizdine alkaloids, which can cause liver damage to some individuals. Never go about casually dosing your dog with herbs any more than you would dose him with a prescription drug. Your dog may have a condition that would make such a dosage dangerous. Consult an expert first.

Herbal medications come in many forms. Probably the most useful is the dried bulk form. Some of these can be added directly to your dog's food. Storage time varies from herb to herb, and lot depends on the way the herb is preserved as well. Read labels carefully, and don't try to store too much.

Homeopathy

Homeopathy has become an important part of alternative veterinary practice. Today there are 1,350 recognized homeopathic remedies. Homeopathy works on a simple, interesting principle: "Like cures like." To cure an illness, you give the patient a very small, diluted amount of a substance that in large amounts would produce symptoms similar to the target disease. The body responds by re-setting its systems to heal itself. The major difference in philosophy between homeopathy and conventional western medicine (which homeopaths call allopathy) is that traditional medicine usually works by introducing a completely different or foreign substance into the body to treat the illness.

Homeopaths believe that this can cause more harm than good: it forces the body to deal with two problems rather than one, and gives the body nothing to stimulate it to heal.

Homeopathic remedies come in pellet or liquid form. The most curious thing about homeopathic remedies concerns the "potency" of the substance, which shouldn't be confused with the "strength" of a conventional drug. In homeopathy, the more diluted the substance is, the greater potency it has. Very potent homeopathic remedies have none of the original "substance" left in them, but I am told that they retain the "energy" from said substances. I confess to not understanding this principle myself, but I have been assured by my homeopathic friends that it works. Always check with a homeopathic vet before administering homeopathic remedies designed for human beings. The dosages and applications may differ.

Homeopathy remedies are almost always given one at a time, and should not be combined with any other therapy, including conventional medicine, acupuncture, herbal treatments, or even another homeopathic remedy. Doing so cancels out the first remedy, and makes things much more difficult to sort out and diagnose. Many homeopathic vets believe that homeopathic remedies can be combined with flower essence therapy (see above). Massage, nutritional therapy, and chiropractic care are also

Herb Hint

Please don't collect herbs in the wild. It's easy to get varieties confused, and some native plants are becoming extremely rare due to over-collection. Buy your herbal medication commercially, and always on the advice of an experienced practitioner.

Alternative therapies shouldn't be used as a replacement for traditional care.

safely used in conjunction with homeopathy. Opinions differ about acupressure. Many homeopathic vets believe it's safe to use with homeopathy, but some disagree.

Never substitute homeopathic home care for qualified veterinary practice. In particular, don't attempt homeopathic remedies for an emergency condition, unless you are on the road to the vet at the same time!

Massage

Massage can speed healing (not on open wounds or broken bones, please). It can be done with a variety of strokes and touch techniques, including effleurage, compression, joint rotation, and tapping, using slow, deliberate movements.

Never administer herbs to your Maltese without consulting an expert.

Reiki (pronounced ray-KEE) is a Japanese technique meaning "spiritually led life energy" is a touch-healing system. It reportedly works by opening the energy centers, or chakras, of the body. It is a complementary therapy not meant to replace traditional healing. If you are interested in learning more about Reiki, visit www.reiki.com or www.reiki.7gen.com.

TTouch therapy is another massage-like technique. It was developed by Linda Tellington-Jones about 40 years ago as a horse therapy. Now it is used on dogs as well. In TTouch, the practitioner (and it can be you) makes gentle clockwise circles, of varying type or pattern, for one and a quarter revolutions on the animal, using slightly curved fingers. Sessions last from 10 to 30 minutes. The most common site is the ear, which helps soothe dogs and fight stress. For ongoing TTouch, you can get a TTouch body-wrap (made with an Ace bandage). Many people combine acupuncture with the TTouch therapy. To learn more about TTouch go to www.lindatellington-jones.com or www.ttouch.com.

FIRST AID AND EMERGENCIES

Of course you'll keep the safety and security of your Maltese in mind throughout his life. However, even the most vigilant owner can't control every situation, and it helps to be prepared just in case your Maltese finds himself in an emergency situation.

Recognizing an Emergency

Get your Maltese to the vet if he shows any of these signs:

- Breathing difficulties
- Trauma or accident (even if you see no outward signs something is wrong)
- Heavy bleeding or severe laceration
- Bleeding from the nose or mouth
- Spurting blood (arterial bleeding)
- Problems with swallowing
- Wounds from encounters with a snake, scorpion, wild sanimal (or has bitten a toad)
- Electrical shock or burn
- Frostbite or hypothermia
- Heat stroke or hyperthermia
- Fever
- Severe pain
- Difficulty or crying while trying to urinate
- Blood in the urine
- Extreme lethargy
- Seizures or disorientation
- Sudden lameness
- Bloat
- Uncontrolled vomiting or diarrhea
- Black, tarry stools
- Protruded rectum
- Suspected poisoning
- Refusal to eat within 48 hours
- Muscle tremors
- Broken bones
- Unusual swellings, especially sudden, hard, or fast-growing ones

Administering Homeopathic Remedies

If you are giving your dog a homeopathic remedy in pill form, be careful not to touch the capsule. Contact with your hand is said to neutralize the remedy. You should also not feed your dog for fifteen minutes or so before administering a homeopathic medication, since tiny food particles in the mouth can interfere with the action of the remedy.

Your Veterinary First-Aid Kit

Making your own first-aid kit is a great way to be prepared for any emergency. Any old box will do—just mark it clearly "First-Aid Kit" in large letters. To the inside of the box lid, tape any special information someone might need about any conditions or

The best thing you can do for your Maltese in an emergency is stay calm.

allergic reactions your Maltese may have. Tape a special card with the name, address, and phone number of your vet. Also write down the use and dosage for each medication your dog is likely to need, so you won't have to try to figure it out during an emergency. You can use a separate card, or write it right on the bottle. The first-aid kit is also a good place to keep a copy of your dog's medical records, including his rabies certificate, directions to the emergency clinic, and phone numbers of the clinic and your vet.

Here's what you'll need for the "ultimate" first-aid kit:

- Activated charcoal (for poisoning)
- Aloe vera (for minor burns)
- Antibiotic cream
- Antibiotic soap or Nolvasan (skin and wound cleanser)
- Baking soda (for burns caused by acids)

- Bandages or New Skin (the latter is especially useful for cuts on paw pads)
- Benadryl (1 to 2 mg per pound [.5 kg] every 8 hours; 2 to four 25 mg tablets every 8 hours)
- Betadine (for treating wounds)
- Canine first-aid manual
- Canine rectal thermometer
- Clinging wrap heat or ice pack
- Epsom salts (for soaking wounds, especially on the feet)
- Eye dropper
- Gauze and cotton pads (to clean and cover wounds)
- Gentle eye wash
- Hydrocortisone cream (for minor inflammation)
- Immodium for diarrhea: 1 mg per 15 pounds [6.8 kg] 1 to 2 times a day, or 1 tbsp for every 10 pounds [4.5 kg] every 6 hours)
- Ipecac or 3 percent hydrogen peroxide (to induce vomiting)
- Magnifying glass
- Milk of magnesia (for constipation: administer with equal amounts of mineral oil)
- Mineral oil (numerous uses, including constipation)
- Petroleum jelly
- Round-tip scissors
- Rubber or latex gloves (to protect your hands and prevent contamination of wounds)
- Saline eye solution and artificial tear gel
- Soft muzzle (injured dogs tend to bite)
- Styptic powder (stops minor bleeding)
- Syringe (without needle) (to apply oral medication)
- Thermal blanket (prevents shock by preserving the dog's body heat)
- Tweezers or hemostat
- Vinegar (for burns caused by alkaloids)
- Witch hazel (insect bites, minor injuries)

Good to Know

To find a good holistic practitioner of any persuasion, consult the American Holistic Veterinary Medical Association at www.altvetmed.com.

Okay, so it seems like a lot to fit into one box. Do the best you can. The more prepared you are for potential emergencies, the more likely your Maltese will be fine.

CPR

If your Maltese has stopped breathing, you'll want to perform CPR. First, check to see if your dog is choking on a foreign object, and remove it if you can. If he is still not breathing even after you remove it, put your dog a firm surface with the left side up. Check for a heartbeat by listening at the spot where the elbow touches the chest. If you hear a heartbeat but the dog is not breathing, close the dog's mouth and place your mouth over the muzzle, breathing directly into his nose until the chest expands. Repeat 12 to 15 times per minute. If there is no pulse, apply heart massage simultaneously. (The heart is located in the lower half of the chest, behind the elbow of the front left leg.) Place one hand below the heart to support the chest. If you have large hands (and because your Maltese is so small), compress the chest with the thumb and forefingers of one hand. Apply heart massage about 100 times per minute. Alternate heart massage with breathing. Sadly, the success of resuscitation is very low, even in skilled hands. But it's worth a try, especially in the case of drowning or electrical shock. Call your veterinarian immediately.

Administering Medication

Medicating a dog is an integral part of both regular and emergency care. The easiest way to give a Maltese a pill is to stick it in a piece of bread or cheese. Sometimes you can just coat the pill in butter. But for those times when this is impossible, it's still not hard to pill your Malty. Simply open the little guy's jaw and place the pills as far back on the tongue as you can. Hold his jaws gently closed, and stroke his throat. Bingo! The pill is gone. You can also try this: while holding the dog's mouth closed, blow gently into his eyes. The natural blink reflex will also cause the dog to swallow the pill.

Liquid medications can be given with an oral syringe, or in a pinch, a turkey baster. Tuck the syringe neatly down the "pocket" of the dog's mouth, and hold the jaws closed, with the lips firmly together. Don't cram the thing directly down your Maltese's throat, because you might get the medication into his lungs by mistake. Keep the dog's head tilted upward. After giving the oral medication, stroke your dog's throat gently.

Emergency Situations

Anaphylactic Shock

Anaphylaxis is a rare, life-threatening, immediate allergic reaction. It is almost always caused by something injected such as

Moving an Injured Dog

If you must move an injured dog, wrap his head in a towel (allowing him, of course, nose room to breathe). This will keep him calm and prevent you from being bitten.

You can make your own canine first-aid kit and keep it in the house for emergencies.

insect stings, antibiotics, and vaccines, although it can very rarely happen with food or other agents in susceptible animals. Unfortunately, there's is no way to predict which dog may have an anaphylactic reaction to what substances

Signs include diarrhea, vomiting, difficulty breathing, shock, seizures, and coma. The dog's gums will be pale, and the legs cold to the touch. His pulse will be fast but weak. If untreated, it results in respiratory and cardiac failure, and death. If your Maltese is having such a reaction, get him to the vet immediately. *Do not wait*. He'll be treated with epinephrine, IV fluids, oxygen, and other medications.

Once you know your dog is susceptible to something like bee stings, your vet can teach you how to give him an injection yourself (perhaps with an epi-pen, a special syringe and needle filled with a single dose of epinephrine) and let you bring the medication home.

Bee, Wasp, and Hornet Stings

While all stings are painful, some are deadly. If your Maltese is allergic to bee stings, he may have trouble breathing or develop hives. Give him a Benadryl and take him to the vet right away. If he does not seem to be having an allergic reaction, scrape out the stinger with a credit card. (Don't try pulling it out, because you can squeeze more poison in.) Apply a cold compress and meat tenderizer to the wound.

Electrical Shock

Chewers that they are, puppies can easily fall victim to electric shock. Most dogs yelp when it happens, and in minor cases you will observe burns on the tongue or roof of the mouth. A more serious shock could travel down to the lungs and damage them as well. And of course, the most serious cases can kill your dog. As always, the best treatment is prevention by encasing exposed cords in PVC pipes or by buying "pet proof" cords that can prevent the shock. You can also spray Bitter Apple over dangerous cords to try and prevent chewing. If your dog receives an electrical shock, he needs a quick trip to the vet. Regard it as an emergency.

Foreign Body Obstruction

Even the delicate Maltese is not above chomping down on something other than his assigned dinner. As a result, any number of unsavory items can get lodged anywhere along the gastrointestinal tract. Some things are too big to leave the stomach; others may make it out of there but get stuck somewhere in the intestines. Most dogs with this problem will have diarrhea (most likely associated with straining to defecate) and vomiting. Other signs include a tense abdomen, lack of appetite, and high temperature, especially if the intestine has been punctured. The most dangerous kind of obstruction may be items like string or yarn than can tie up a considerable portion of the intestine and even cut through it. Your vet will need to take x-rays or perhaps run some barium through the dog to make a diagnosis and decide on the course of treatment, which usually includes surgery.

Heat Stroke (Hyperthermia)

Unfortunately for your Maltese, he lacks those all so wonderful sweat glands that help keep you cool in the summer. Well, he does have a few, mostly in the footpads where they really aren't that helpful. To cool off during the sultry days of summer, your Maltese needs to pant (inelegant as that sounds), although he can also dissipate some heat by dilating bloods vessels in the ears and on the face. It is frighteningly easy for a dog to overheat—even excessive play will do it. Normally your dog's body temperature runs between 100.5 and 102.5°F (38 to 39°C). If his temperature goes up to 106 or 107°F (41 to 41.5°C), it's called heat exhaustion. If it rises to 107°F (41.5°C), it's heat stroke, and potentially fatal due to brain damage.

Signs of heat stroke include:

- Lethargy
- Bright red tongue and gums
- Panting
- Vomiting
- Seizure
- Collapse
- Disorientation, confusion

If this happens to your Maltese, pour cool (not ice-cold) water on him and wrap him in cool wet towels. Then take him to the vet.

Hypothermia

Maltese are small dogs, and can't tolerate extreme cold very well. Dogs can be frostbitten just the same as people can, and the worst effects show up on the same places—the digits, ears, and the tip of the nose. Severe cases of frostbite require amputation. In the earliest stages, the skin appears pale or gray; later it becomes red and inflamed. A gentle compress of warm water may help mild cases, but more severely affected dogs can suffer serious tissue damage. Don't try to massage the area—you can cause more tissue damage. Try to keep your dog from licking or chewing the affected area also. Your veterinarian may want to prescribe analgesics for the pain.

If your Maltese is allergic to bee stings, emergency care will be necessary.

Poisoning

So many substances can cause poisoning in so many ways that it is impossible to give general directions. Here's what you can do:

- Get in touch with a veterinarian or a poison control center, and follow their instructions. The ASPCA National Animal Poison Control (800-548-2423 or 900-680-0000) will dispense telephone help for poisoned animals. There is a fee per call, so get out your credit card. Don't try to medicate your pet until you talk to a professional. Have at hand all the evidence you can muster

Good to Know

Do not give your Maltese Tylenol, ibuprofin, or aspirin, all of which are dangerous to dogs.

about the material your Maltese has eaten.

- If that is not possible, and the suspected poisoning occurred within the past three hours, induce vomiting (unless your Malty has ingested a petroleum product, a cleaning solution, or a strong acid or alkali). In general, try to induce vomiting in your dog if he has consumed any of the following: acetone, alcohol, antifreeze, diazinon, drugs, insecticides, lead, or rat poison. To induce vomiting, give your dog a tablespoon of hydrogen peroxide every ten minutes until the dog vomits, and then take him to your vet. If you have no hydrogen peroxide, use a teaspoon of salt or a tablespoon of dry mustard. Syrup of ipecac also works, but takes about half an hour. Use the hydrogen peroxide if possible. Do not give any other liquid.
- If the poison is a petroleum product, cleaning solution, strong acid, or strong alkali, or was ingested more than 3 hours ago, you must get the dog to a vet right away. Do not induce vomiting if the dog has eaten: Bleach, cleaners, cleaning fluid, fertilizers, furniture polish, gasoline, kerosene, paint thinner, or pine oil.
- If the pet vomits, save a sample of the vomitus in a sealable plastic bag for the vet to examine.

Skunked!

While Maltese aren't likely to go charging around the yard after skunks, any dog who is out at night is vulnerable to this sort of mishap. Skunk spray is a smelly, oily material produced by glands located near the anus of the skunk. It's active ingredient is an organic compound called mercaptan whose main component is sulfur. (It's the same stuff that is added to natural gas to make it smell badly when there's a leak.) There is just no reason to want this stuff on your dog.

Unless the dog gets it right in his eyes (in which case call your vet) the effects aren't dangerous—just extremely unpleasant. It's your job to deodorize your dog. Trying to mask the stuff with shampoo or perfumes won't work. Tomato juice has its adherents, but doesn't work either. You can try bathing your dog in a

Grass Awns and Your Dog

These nasty weed seeds can penetrate your dog's skin and imbed in his eyes, paws, or nose. If you can readily see the awn in the skin, you can pull it out. However, the awn can imbed itself far up the nose or under the third eyelid, making the dog sneeze uncontrollably or paw at his head. His eye may also look infected.

Years ago, I noticed a red swollen eye on one of my dogs. I happened to have some people-doctors at my house, and I showed it them. They looked and looked and saw nothing—completely stumped. So I took the dog to the vet, who removed the awn and said, "Tell your doctor friends to look under the third eyelid next time." I did, and they said blankly, "Third eyelid? Dogs have an extra eyelid?" They do indeed. C'est la différence.

Your small dog is sensitive to extreme weather—both hot and cold.

mixture of 1 quart of three-percent hydrogen peroxide, 1 cup baking soda and 1 teaspoon liquid dish soap. Then rinse. Your best bet, though, is a product specifically made to neutralize the odor of skunk spray, such as Skunk Off, which can be purchased at a pet supply store.

Snakebites

Although there is no actual data about how many dogs are killed by venomous snakes each year, it does happen. If a snake does bite your Malty, stay calm. Don't grab a knife, make an X, and start sucking at the (probably) non-existent venom. Even when a venomous snakes bites, it does not always release its venom, which is a precious commodity. In a warning strike, it does not inject venom. To avoid snakebite, keep your dog on a leash in strange areas, and do not let him dig or explore holes or beneath woodpiles—a favorite snake hideout, since woodpiles attract mice, a snake's favorite food. Most snakes are more active at night, especially in warmer weather. If you live in an area where there are poisonous snakes, and that includes every state except Maine, Hawaii, and most of Alaska, learn to identify them. This helps not only in steering clear of them, but in recognizing harmless snakes that are helpful to the environment. If your dog is bitten, take him to a veterinarian immediately. Call ahead, so the vet can get the necessary antivenin from the hospital. Most vets don't keep the stuff on hand.

THE SENIOR MALTESE

Dogs are living longer lives these days, with many Maltese getting a peek at their late teens. Older dogs suffer from most of the same aging signs the rest of us face: they get gray; sleep more than they did as adults; and, lose some hearing and vision. You can't do much about these things, but you can certainly take care of the single most common problem that older dogs face: dental disease. This is particularly common in toy dogs, who tend to have more crowded teeth. Dental disease begins with plaque. If you don't brush it away, it hardens into to tartar. Tartar buildup leads directly to gum disease and tooth loss. Gum disease invites bacterial invasion that can even attack the internal organs such as the kidneys. To prevent this from happening, brush your Malty's teeth every day. If you haven't been doing this, take him to your vet for a professional cleaning job and then brush his teeth every day afterwards, right after you brush you own.

One problem of older pets can be congestive heart failure (first noticed as moist coughing during the night or shortness of breath). There's no cure for the condition, but there is medical treatment that can lengthen your dog's life. Other diseases of old age include hypertension, glaucoma, inflammatory bowel disease, chronic liver disease, and Cushing's disease. A very common nerve disorder affecting older dogs is "old dog vestibular disease," in which a nerve malfunctions within the balance mechanism of the inner ear. The dog may walk in circles with his head tilted. Usually the condition cures itself within a few weeks to months, although some head tilting may remain. Check with your vet, of course. Older dogs are more likely to develop both benign skin tumors and cancer. Early examination and treatment of all lumps is the key. Older pets also suffer from arthritis and obesity, both treatable! Older dogs should be put on a diet that suits their changing health requirements (more high-quality protein, fewer calories).

Housetraining problems may crop up again. The cause may be a disease like diabetes, or it may occur as the kidneys lose their ability to concentrate urine, which makes your Maltese drink and urinate more frequently to rid the body of waste problems. Older dogs can also suffer from canine cognitive dysfunction, a disease similar to Alzheimer's in people. Dogs with this condition may seem confused, lose housetraining, and be uninterested in petting. However, there is medication and special prescription diets for this disease. In addition, several companies make diaper-type pants for incontinent dogs. Make sure you select the right fit and change the pant frequently so the moisture does not collect against the dog's delicate skin.

Be sure you know where the nearest emergency veterinary clinic is located.

Healthy older dogs thrive on regular moderate exercise, so don't neglect this critical element of dog care. And never ever assume that your dog's medical problems are "just a part of getting older" and that no treatment is possible. Often, there is, so talk to your vet.

Sadly, the time may come when you have to make the difficult decision about letting your beloved pet go. Your final act of kindness may be to ease the pain of your long-time friend. But until you need to contemplate such a profound decision, give your senior citizen a little extra care, understanding, and attention. Savor your dog's golden years. May they be many and memorable.

Age-Proofing Checklist

- Train your Maltese using both voice and hand commands to ensure that your dog will always respond—even if he begins to lose his sight or hearing.
- Keep to a daily routine. Older (and younger) dogs find comfort in knowing what to expect.
- Brush your dog's teeth daily.
- Don't move too quickly into your Maltese's space or make sudden movements that might startle him.
- If necessary, give your dog more frequent bathroom breaks. If your Maltese has arthritis, make sure he has a warm place to sleep, and avoid activities that stress those old joints.
- If your older dog is in good overall health, get involved (together) in moderate exercise.

Pill Tip

If you have to break a scored tablet in half, put it on a flat, hard surface, and place a thumb on each side of the score. Then press down with both thumbs. This works well with any pill that has a rounded surface.

- Match your dog's caloric intake with his level of activity.
- Frequently bathe and groom your dog. As dogs age, their skin glands produce less oil, which increases the chances of dry, flaky skin and matted hair.
- Take your Maltese in for semi-annual veterinary checkups, or more often if he has an on-going medical condition.

THE END OF LIFE: KNOWING WHEN IT'S TIME

Anesthesia and the Senior Dog

It's a myth that anesthesia is particularly dangerous for an older dog. With the new short acting anesthesthetics available nowadays, it is remarkably safe—much, much safer than letting your Maltese get dental disease. The same goes for removing suspicous lumps.

Even the Maltese cannot live forever. And the saddest duty of every loving dog owner is seeing his pet through the gate into the other world, whatever it may be. If you are struggling with this decision, remember you are not alone. It's also comforting to know that your pet will actually help make the decision for you, by telling you he needs to leave.

The first clue is a change in his routine. When he no longer seems to have any zest for life, when his appetite is gone and he doesn't seem to want to go out for walks any more, when the kisses stop, you can know that his mind is on higher things. He may also be in pain beyond the reach of medication. Other factors that may help you decide are incontinence, extreme expense or extraordinarily high level of care. Most of us gladly sacrifice time and money for your pets when there is a hope of a cure, but when it goes only to prolonging a death, we know that the wisest and indeed the kindest thing is to say good-bye.

Of course, you will grieve after your pet is gone. This is natural—don't listen to anyone who says "It's only a dog" or any other such thoughtless remark. Give yourself both time and permission to grieve. Doing so confirms your membership in the circle of those who can extend their love and caring beyond themselves to others—even if the others are of a different species.

Just as with human beings, you can have your pet cremated or buried in a pet cemetery. Some people prefer to bring the ashes home and scatter them over a favorite meadow. No matter what you decide, you will know that your Maltese's gentle, joyous spirit will live on in your heart forever.

Did You Know?

All older pets should have a general checkup twice each year.

Once your Maltese enters his senior years, you should make twice-yearly trips to the vet.

The Next Step

People have diametrically opposed ways of dealing with pet loss. Some people want to get a new dog immediately. Some need a period of months or years to grieve before they can bring themselves to get another dog. Go with your own feelings and what you know is right. In the meantime you can memorialize your dog by making a scrapbook, writing a poem, and contributing to your local shelter or Maltese Rescue in his name.

Sooner or later, I promise you, you will acknowledge the hole in your heart that only a Maltese can fill. Somewhere—at a show or in a shelter, a certain pair of bright dark eyes will catch your heart and take your breath away. And you'll know it's time—time once again to embark upon the glorious adventure of owning a Maltese.

AKC MALTESE BREED STANDARD

General Appearance: The Maltese is a toy dog covered from head to foot with a mantle of long, silky, white hair. He is gentle-mannered and affectionate, eager and sprightly in action, and, despite his size, possessed of the vigor needed for the satisfactory companion.

Head: Of medium length and in proportion to the size of the dog. The skull is slightly rounded on top, the stop moderate. The drop ears are rather low set and heavily feathered with long hair that hangs close to the head. Eyes are set not too far apart; they are very dark and round, their black rims enhancing the gentle yet alert expression. The muzzle is of medium length, fine and tapered but not snipy. The nose is black. The teeth meet in an even, edge-to-edge bite, or in a scissors bite.

Neck: Sufficient length of neck is desirable as promoting a high carriage of the head.

Body: Compact, the height from the withers to the ground equaling the length from the withers to the root of the tail. Shoulder blades are sloping, the elbows well knit and held close to the body. The back is level in topline, the ribs well sprung. The chest is fairly deep, the loins taut, strong, and just slightly tucked up underneath.

Tail: A long-haired plume carried gracefully over the back, its tip lying to the side over the quarter.

Legs and Feet: Legs are fine-boned and nicely feathered. Forelegs are straight, their pastern joints well knit and devoid of appreciable bend. Hind legs are strong and moderately angulated at stifles and hocks. The feet are small and round, with toe pads black. Scraggly hairs on the feet may be trimmed to give a neater appearance.

Coat and Color: The coat is single, that is, without undercoat. It hangs long, flat, and silky over the sides of the body almost, if not quite, to the ground. The long head-hair may be tied up in a topknot or it may be left hanging. Any suggestion of kinkiness, curliness, or woolly texture is objectionable. Color, pure white. Light tan or lemon on the ears is permissible, but not desirable.

Size: Weight under 7 pounds, with from 4 to 6 pounds preferred. Overall quality is to be favored over size.

Gait: The Maltese moves with a jaunty, smooth, flowing gait. Viewed from the side, he gives an impression of rapid movement, size considered. In the stride, the forelegs reach straight and free from the shoulders, with elbows close. Hind legs to move in a straight line. Cowhocks or any suggestion of hind leg toeing in or out are faults.

Temperament: For all his diminutive size, the Maltese seems to be without fear. His trust and affectionate responsiveness are very appealing. He is among the gentlest mannered of all little dogs, yet he is lively and playful as well as vigorous.

Approved March 10, 1964

KENNEL CLUB BREED STANDARD

General Appearance: Smart, white-coated dog, with proud head carriage.

Characteristics: Lively, intelligent, alert.

Temperament: Sweet-tempered.

Head and Skull: From stop to centre of skull (centre between forepart of ears) and stop to tip of nose, equally balanced. Stop well defined. Nose black. Muzzle broad, well filled under eye. Not snipey.

Eyes: Oval, not bulging, dark brown, black eye rims, with dark haloes.

Ears: Long, well feathered, hanging close to head; hair to mingle with coat at shoulders.

Mouth: Jaws strong, with perfect, regular and complete scissor bite, i.e. upper teeth closely overlapping lower teeth and set square to the jaws. Teeth even.

Neck: Medium length.

Forequarters: Legs short and straight. Shoulders well sloped.

Body: Well balanced, essentially short and cobby. Good spring of rib, back level from withers to tail.

Hindquarters: Legs short, well angulated.

Feet: Round, pads black.

Tail: Feathered, carried well arched over back.

Gait/Movement: Straight and free-flowing, without weaving. Viewed from behind, legs should neither be too close nor too wide apart.

Coat: Good length, not impeding action, straight, of silky texture, never woolly. Never crimped and without woolly undercoat.

Colour: Pure white, but slight lemon markings permissible.

Size: Height not exceeding 25 cms (10 ins) from ground to withers.

Faults: Any departure from the foregoing points should be considered a fault and the seriousness with which the fault should be regarded should be in exact proportion to its degree and its effect upon the health and welfare of the dog.

Note: Male animals should have two apparently normal testicles fully descended into the scrotum.
September 2000

RESOURCES

ASSOCIATIONS AND ORGANIZATIONS

BREED CLUBS

American Kennel Club (AKC)
5580 Centerview Drive
Raleigh, NC 27606
Telephone: (919) 233-9767
Fax: (919) 233-3627
E-mail: info@akc.org
www.akc.org

American Maltese Association
Corresponding Secretary:
Barbara Miener
2523 N. Starr Street
Tacoma, WA 98403
www.americanmaltese.org

Canadian Kennel Club (CKC)
89 Skyway Avenue, Suite 100
Etobicoke, Ontario M9W 6R4
Telephone: (416) 675-5511
Fax: (416) 675-6506
E-mail: information@ckc.ca
www.ckc.ca

Federation Cynologique Internationale (FCI)
Secretariat General de la FCI
Place Albert 1er, 13
B – 6530 Thuin
Belqique
www.fci.be

The Kennel Club
1 Clarges Street
London
W1J 8AB
Telephone: 0870 606 6750
Fax: 0207 518 1058
www.the-kennel-club.org.uk

United Kennel Club (UKC)
100 E. Kilgore Road
Kalamazoo, MI 49002-5584
Telephone: (269) 343-9020
Fax: (269) 343-7037
E-mail: pbickell@ukcdogs.com
www.ukcdogs.com

PET SITTERS

National Association of Professional Pet Sitters
15000 Commerce Parkway, Suite C
Mt. Laurel, New Jersey 08054
Telephone: (856) 439-0324
Fax: (856) 439-0525
E-mail: napps@ahint.com
www.petsitters.org

Pet Sitters International
201 East King Street
King, NC 27021-9161
Telephone: (336) 983-9222
Fax: (336) 983-5266
E-mail: info@petsit.com
www.petsit.com

RESCUE ORGANIZATIONS AND ANIMAL WELFARE GROUPS

American Humane Association (AHA)
63 Inverness Drive East
Englewood, CO 80112
Telephone: (303) 792-9900
Fax: 792-5333
www.americanhumane.org

American Society for the Prevention of Cruelty to Animals (ASPCA)
424 E. 92nd Street
New York, NY 10128-6804
Telephone: (212) 876-7700
www.aspca.org

Royal Society for the Prevention of Cruelty to Animals (RSPCA)
Telephone: 0870 3335 999
Fax: 0870 7530 284
www.rspca.org.uk

The Humane Society of the United States (HSUS)
2100 L Street, NW
Washington DC 20037
Telephone: (202) 452-1100
www.hsus.org

SPORTS

Canine Freestyle Federation, Inc.
Secretary: Brandy Clymire
E-Mail: secretary@canine-freestyle.org
www.canine-freestyle.org

International Agility Link (IAL)
Global Administrator: Steve Drinkwater
E-mail: yunde@powerup.au
www.agilityclick.com/~ial

North American Dog Agility Council
11522 South Hwy 3
Cataldo, ID 83810
www.nadac.com

United States Dog Agility Association
P.O. Box 850955
Richardson, TX 75085-0955
Telephone: (972) 487-2200
www.usdaa.com

World Canine Freestyle Organization
P.O. Box 350122
Brooklyn, NY 11235-2525
Telephone: (718) 332-8336
www.worldcaninefreestyle.org

THERAPY

Delta Society
875 124th Ave NE, Suite 101
Bellevue, WA 98005
Telephone: (425) 226-7357
Fax: (425) 235-1076
E-mail: info@deltasociety.org
www.deltasociety.org

Therapy Dogs International (TDI)
88 Bartley Road
Flanders, NJ 07836
Telephone: (973) 252-9800
Fax: (973) 252-7171
E-mail: tdi@gti.net
www.tdi-dog.org

TRAINING

Association of Pet Dog Trainers (APDT)
150 Executive Center Drive
Box 35
Greenville, SC 29615
Telephone: (800) PET-DOGS
Fax: (864) 331-0767
E-mail:
information@apdt.com
www.apdt.com

National Association of Dog Obedience Instructors
PMB 369
729 Grapevine Hwy.
Hurst, TX 76054-2085
www.nadoi.org

VETERINARY AND HEALTH RESOURCES

Academy of Veterinary Homeopathy (AVH)
P.O. Box 9280
Wilmington, DE 19809
Telephone: (866) 652-1590
Fax: (866) 652-1590
E-mail: office@TheAVH.org
www.theavh.org

American Academy of Veterinary Acupuncture (AAVA)
100 Roscommon Drive, Suite 320
Middletown, CT 06457
Telephone: (860) 635-6300
Fax: (860) 635-6400
E-mail: office@aava.org
www.aava.org

American Animal Hospital Association (AAHA)
P.O. Box 150899
Denver, CO 80215-0899
Telephone: (303) 986-2800
Fax: (303) 986-1700
E-mail: info@aahanet.org
www.aahanet.org/index.cfm

American College of Veterinary Internal Medicine (ACVIM)
1997 Wadsworth Blvd., Suite A
Lakewood, CO 80214-5293
Telephone: (800) 245-9081
Fax: (303) 231-0880
Email: ACVIM@ACVIM.org
www.acvim.org

American College of Veterinary Ophthalmologists (ACVO)
P.O. Box 1311
Meridian, Idaho 83860
Telephone: (208) 466-7624
Fax: (208) 466-7693
E-mail: office@acvo.com
www.acvo.com

American Holistic Veterinary Medical Association (AHVMA)
2218 Old Emmorton Road
Bel Air, MD 21015
Telephone: (410) 569-0795
Fax: (410) 569-2346
E-mail: office@ahvma.org
www.ahvma.org

American Veterinary Medical Association (AVMA)
1931 North Meacham Road – Suite 100
Schaumburg, IL 60173
Telephone: (847) 925-8070
Fax: (847) 925-1329
E-mail: avmainfo@avma.org
www.avma.org

ASPCA Animal Poison Control Center
1717 South Philo Road, Suite 36
Urbana, IL 61802
Telephone: (888) 426-4435
www.aspca.org

British Veterinary Association (BVA)
7 Mansfield Street
London
W1G 9NQ
Telephone: 020 7636 6541
Fax: 020 7436 2970
E-mail: bvahq@bva.co.uk
www.bva.co.uk

Canine Eye Registration Foundation (CERF) VMDB/CERF
1248 Lynn Hall
625 Harrison St.
Purdue University
West Lafayette, IN 47907-2026
Telephone: (765) 494-8179
E-mail: CERF@vmbd.org
www.vmdb.org

Orthopedic Foundation for Animals (OFA)
2300 NE Nifong Blvd
Columbus, Missouri 65201-3856
Telephone: (573) 442-0418
Fax: (573) 875-5073
Email: ofa@offa.org
www.offa.org

DEDICATION
To Fred and Cindy Revell

ABOUT THE AUTHOR
Diane Morgan is an award-winning writer who is the author of many books, including *Good Dogkeeping*, *The Simple Guide to Choosing a Dog*, and *Feeding Your Dog for Life*. She is an ardent supporter of canine rescue and a charter member and Treasurer of Basset Hound Rescue of Old Dominion. She is a college professor of philosophy and literature and resides in Williamsport, Maryland with seven dogs, two humans, and an uncounted number of goldfish.

Photo Credits

Photos on pages 54, 61, 65, 110, 113 courtesy of Paulette Braun

Photos on pages 11, 30, 108, 181 courtesy of Robert Pearcy

All other photos courtesy of Isabelle Francais